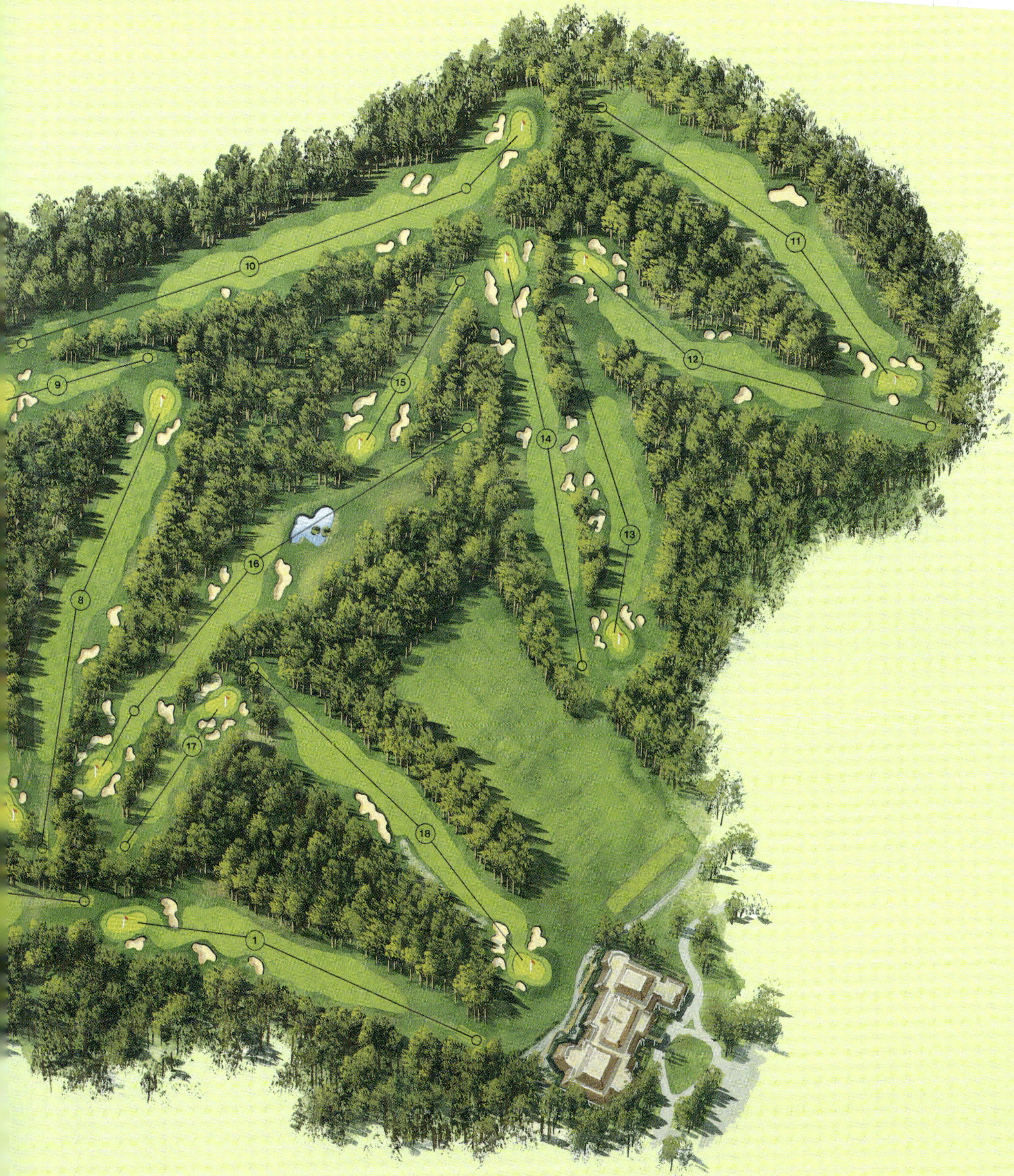
10
11
9
15
12
14
13
16
8
17
18
1

105th U.S. OPEN
Pinehurst

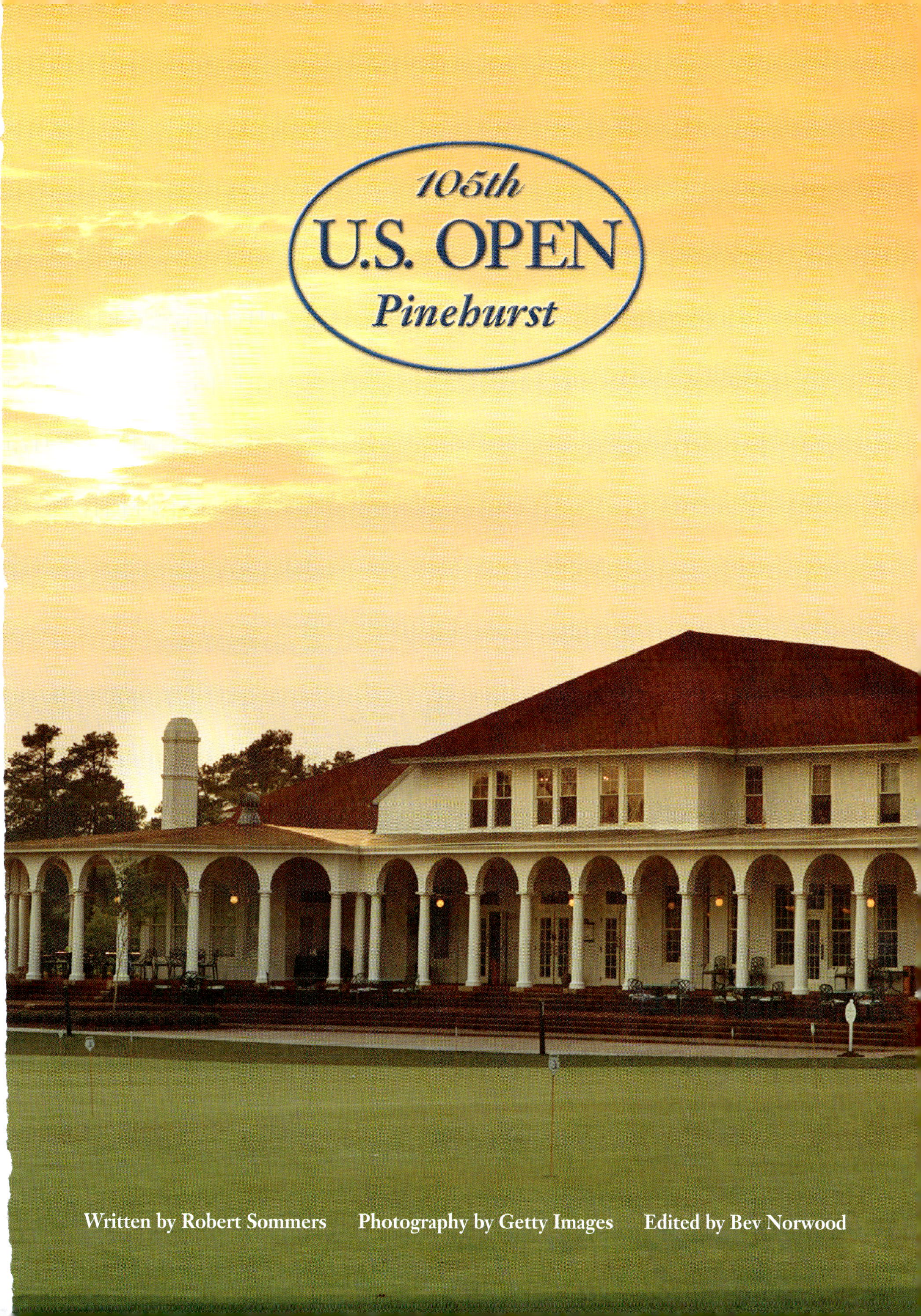

Written by Robert Sommers   Photography by Getty Images   Edited by Bev Norwood

ISBN 1-878843-42-7

©2005 United States Golf Association®
Golf House, Far Hills, N.J. 07931

Statistics produced by Unisys Corporation

Photographs ©Getty Images except as noted
Photographs on pages 5, 13 and 14 ©USGA/John Mummert
Course illustrations by Dan Wardlaw © The Majors of Golf

Published by IMG Worldwide Inc.,
1360 East Ninth Street, Cleveland, Ohio 44114

Designed and produced by Davis Design

Printed in the United States of America

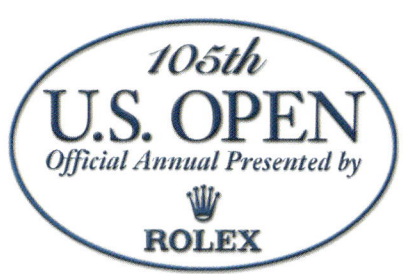

While Michael Campbell's victory in the 105th U.S. Open Championship was unexpected, the final score and the rigorous test that Pinehurst No. 2 visited upon the 156 contestants did not surprise me at all. By reputation and past history, a 72-hole score hovering around par on the famed course was anticipated.

As it turned out, I had the opportunity to play No. 2 on the eve of tournament week and the course was everything that I had anticipated it would be. When I walked off the 18th green that Saturday afternoon, I was confident that any red numbers that appeared on the leaderboards over the next seven days would be in the low single digits and might well all disappear by week's end.

I knew that the tight fairways, the lush, punishing Bermuda rough and Pinehurst's intimidating, inverted-bowl-shaped greens would ensure the prized sanctity of one of the most prestigious of all American courses. I knew that it would take a steady, deliberate, patient player to capture our national championship and Michael Campbell proved to be that type of competitor that week in North Carolina.

All due credit goes to the New Zealander for achieving the greatest victory of his career in the face of the challenge of Tiger Woods, who was to come up just short of adding the second leg in his quest for professional golf's never-achieved same-season Grand Slam.

The U.S. Open instantly elevated Campbell to hero status in his native country as he became just the second New Zealander to own one of golf's major championships, joining Bob Charles 42 years after the lefthander won the British Open.

Rolex is proud to present this 21st official annual as a chronicle of another exceptional U.S. Open.

Arnold Palmer

The first hole, par 4 and 401 yards.

A stroll through the village of Pinehurst is like a tour of the Williamsburg maze. Streets wander aimlessly, some circle back on themselves and occasionally change names in mid-stride. One follows a sweeping path that heads out of the village, then curls back into its heart. Two others form a horseshoe, encircling both the town library and the village chapel, which claims as its first clergyman Edward Everett Hale, the author of the short story "The Man Without A Country."

Described universally as quaint, the village, although dotted with a growing number of real estate agencies, has held its charm. It has the usual stores: the ambitiously named department store, the mandatory gift shop, an assortment of restaurants — the Magnolia Inn and Theo's among them — jewelry shops, women's shops, banks, the town theater, law offices, of course, and another shop of uncertain lineage that displays a scoring standard usually carried by young boys at golf tournaments. This one shows Tiger Woods at 12 under par and Ernie Els at three over. Obviously someone's partial.

As tasteful as ever, the Holly Inn, the Manor Inn and the Pine Crest cluster close together, not far from the elegant Carolina Hotel, the town's grande dame. Painted pure white under a bronzed roof, The Carolina sits at the center of Pinehurst's traffic pattern. Nattily dressed attendants greet guests and guide them to the entranceway that leads through the lobby to the check-in desk. Though not as prominent as in earlier times, the jigsaw puzzle is still a part of The Carolina's rites. Passing guests commonly pause to fit in a piece or two.

The Putter Boy was sculpted in 1912.

Carolina Vista Drive leads from the hotel's main entrance directly to the Pinehurst Country Club, with its colonnaded clubhouse and its first five courses (three others occupy nearby land). One of golf's jewels, Pinehurst No. 2 stands at the top level of American courses. Some with broad knowledge of the game believe it's the best of them all.

In June of 2005, the United States Open Championship returned to No. 2 for an encore. It made its Open debut in 1999, a championship remembered as the last tournament Payne Stewart won. Four months later he and five others died in a plane crash in South Dakota.

As everything else, Pinehurst's clubhouse has changed over the years. It's grown larger, and carpeting covers what had been the bare wooden floors of the big lobby. Now the lobby is a dining room presided over by a formally dressed majordomo.

But the same old pictures still line the long hallway of the clubhouse — Gene Sarazen, Walter Hagen, Jimmy Thomson, Wild Bill Mehlhorn, his name still spelled wrong, Byron Nelson, Sam Snead standing beside Jimmy Steed, an old caddie,

Statues of Donald Ross (left) and Richard Tufts.

Payne Stewart's victory is commemorated here.

Ben Hogan and the 1951 Ryder Cup teams of both the United States and of Britain and Ireland.

A window display honors Payne Stewart, and outside a bronze statue captures the moment his winning putt fell. Lifelike bronzes of Donald Ross and Richard Tufts stand nearby, not on pedestals but side-by-side on a red brick walkway as if they had stopped to chat. So natural are they, you could easily say hello passing by.

Two of the more significant men the game has known, Tufts and Ross earned their prominence. While Ross is generally considered among the greatest of all golf course designers, it is difficult to imagine anyone who, in his time, influenced the game more than Richard S. Tufts. A Harvard-educated proper New Englander, Dick Tufts was the grandson of Pinehurst's founder, James Tufts. He ran Pinehurst during its glory years in the middle of the 20th century, but more than that, his knowledge of the game and passion for its principles reached beyond most men who had spent their lifetimes in golf administration. Tufts served on USGA committees from 1936 through 1971, and over those 35 years he held the chairmanship of nearly every one of them. Because of his devotion and effectiveness, he rose to the offices of secretary, vice president, and in 1956 and 1957 served two terms as president.

Known in Pinehurst as Mr. Richard, he made his major impact dealing with the rules of golf and championships. Overall, his achievements seem staggering. Frank Hannigan, an old USGA hand, credits him with just about everything good the USGA accomplished during his time. He re-organized the Green Section into a group of agronomists who visit clubs and analyze and advise on golf course maintenance, he revised the handicap system, he was behind adding junior championships to the USGA's menu, and with Joe Dey, for many years the USGA's executive director, he developed the USGA's system of setting up courses for championships, prompted by overly harsh conditions during the early 1950s. In 1958 he helped form the World Amateur Golf Council (now the Inter-

1st
PAR 4
401 YARDS

been accepted by all golfers throughout the world.

While Dick Tufts stood at the heart and soul of the game, Pinehurst and its golf courses stood at his heart and soul. He loved the place and what it stood for — golf in its purest form. When his father, Leonard Tufts, became ill during the 1930s, Mr. Richard took over as Pinehurst's president and chairman. Under his management, Pinehurst reached the height of its prestige, particularly with its series of North and South championships for professionals as well as amateurs, and for women as well as for men.

national Golf Federation), the body that conducts the World Amateur Team Championships.

In perhaps his major accomplishment, Tufts pushed the USGA and the Royal and Ancient Golf Club of St. Andrews to compromise on a universal code of rules. In 1951 the two bodies did indeed agree on a joint set of rules for the game. They went into effect in 1952, and although the rules have changed over the last 53 years, they've

2nd
PAR 4
469 YARDS

3rd
PAR 4
336 YARDS

During its 50-year life the North and South Open drew a field as strong as any in golf. Its roster of champions ranges from Byron Nelson, Ben Hogan and Sam Snead back to Alex Ross, Donald's brother, the winner of the 1907 U.S. Open; Jim Barnes, winner of the first PGA Championship, in 1916, along with the 1921 Open; Fred McLeod, 1908 Open champion; and Walter Hagen, who won everything.

Hogan's successes actually began with the 1940 North and South Open. Until he beat Sam Snead by three strokes that March, he had never won a tournament. Within the next 10 days he won twice more, in Greensboro and in Asheville, in the mountains of western North Carolina — three tournaments in 13 days (36-hole days were com-

The fourth hole, par 5 and 565 yards.

mon then, and tournaments rarely ran from Thursday through Sunday). Hogan was on his way.

The North and South Amateur, meanwhile, lists among its champions Francis Ouimet, Walter Travis, Chick Evans, Bill Campbell, Billy Joe Patton, Curtis Strange, Davis Love III and George Dunlap, who won six of them from 1933 through 1942. As confirmation of the tournament's standing, Jack Nicklaus passed up the 1959 NCAA championship to play in, and win, the North and South. Years later, in one of his proudest moments, Jack watched his son Jack II add his name to the roll of champions.

Its women's champions are equally impressive: Elaine Rosenthal, perhaps best known for her Red Cross fundraising tour with Bob Jones, Perry Adair and Alexa Stirling during the First World War, Stirling herself, Dorothy Campbell Hurd, Glenna Collett, Estelle Lawson Page, Louise Suggs, Babe Zaharias, Barbara McIntire, Marlene Streit, Hollis Stacy, Carol Semple Thompson and Ann Sander.

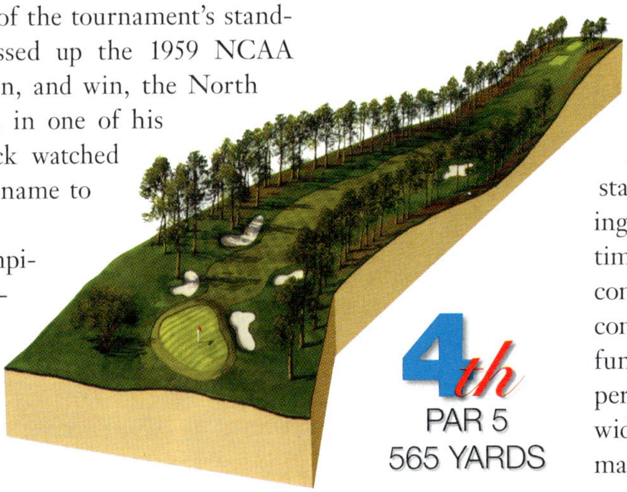

Normally soft-spoken and gentlemanly, Tufts occasionally showed flashes of steel. Upset during his term as USGA president because Augusta National tolerated high-stakes betting on the Masters, he forbid USGA staff members from officiating the tournament. Another time he grew impatient with committee members who complained that the USGA's functions, and those who performed them, weren't widely known. He insisted it mattered little that the asso-

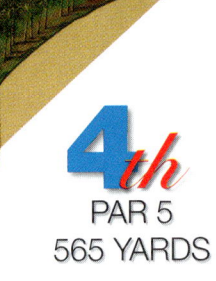

4th
PAR 5
565 YARDS

5th PAR 4 472 YARDS

6th PAR 3 220 YARDS

7th PAR 4 404 YARDS

ciation was not known so long as it was effective.

Then there was the 1951 North and South Open.

The Ryder Cup Match hadn't nearly the standing of later times, and the PGA, the Ryder Cup's parent, often scrambled for sites. As a token of support, Tufts offered No. 2 for the Ryder Cup, and for the players' convenience, scheduled the North and South Open for the following week.

As prize money went, the North and South didn't top the list. Others offered $10,000 to $15,000, but they played for $7,500 at Pinehurst. To spare the players their expenses, though, Tufts put them up at The Carolina, which included their meals, at no charge. That wasn't good enough. The Ryder Cup over, the U.S. team skipped town. Tommy Bolt won, and when it ended, Tufts canceled the North and South Open. It had been played consistently through two world wars, but it ended badly.

It pained Tufts to drop the tournament, but he felt he had been betrayed. Nineteen years later he felt betrayed once again, with more serious consequences.

Tufts shared ownership of Pinehurst with his two brothers and a sister, along with a fifth partner, the son of Isham Sledge, a name more at home in a Trollope novel. Sledge had died and his son wanted nothing of Pinehurst but its financial worth. Dick's brothers sided with Sledge and forced the sale to Diamondhead Corporation, which later events showed had no respect for No. 2. The sale broke Tufts's heart.

Shortly afterward his health failed and he died in 1980 at the age of 84.

A low-handicap golfer in his early years (at his best he played to 4), Tufts had learned the game from Donald Ross, among the most versatile of men. An excellent player, Ross not only won three North and South Opens, he placed fifth in the 1903 United States Open. A tough businessman and administrator, he managed the Pinehurst Country Club while at the same time acting as the club professional, clubmaker and caddiemaster.

Above all, though, Donald Ross ranks as perhaps the best designer of golf courses ever to practice the art. A Scottish immigrant, he not only gave us many of our finest courses, he set standards that define how others in the craft should be measured. He laid out so many courses it is hard to grasp the extent of his works. Ross is said to have designed or revised more than 600. It's probably an exaggeration, because nobody can be sure how many he simply sketched on paper without ever having stepped on or seen the ground. Ross often cringed at the results.

By contrast, many of those he actually worked on at the site are among our very best. He laid out Inverness, the host club of four U.S. Opens, Oak Hill, where Cary Middlecoff, Lee Trevino and Curtis Strange won U.S. Opens, Interlachen Country Club, where Bob Jones won his last Open, and East Lake in Atlanta, where Jones learned to play. He also designed

8th
PAR 4
467 YARDS

9th
PAR 3
175 YARDS

Golf Club in North Palm Beach.

Above all, though, Ross is best remembered for creating the great No. 2 course at Pinehurst, the site of the 1936 PGA Championship, the 1951 Ryder Cup Match, the 1962 U.S. Amateur, the 1994 U.S. Senior Open and the 1999 U.S. Open, along with the long series of North and South championships.

When Bob Jones chose Alister MacKenzie to design the course that was to become Augusta National, Ross threw his creative energies into refining No. 2. He had begun the first nine holes almost from

Scioto Country Club in Columbus, Ohio, where Jones won the 1926 Open and where Jack Nicklaus learned to play; Oakland Hills Country Club, near Detroit, where Ben Hogan shot a majestic 67 in 1951, his finest Open round; the original Hermitage Country Club in Richmond, where Sam Snead won the second of his three PGA Championships; Aronimink Country Club near Philadelphia, where Gary Player won the 1962 PGA; and two priceless gems along Florida's Atlantic Coast — Gulf Stream in Delray Beach and the impeccable Seminole

10th
PAR 5
607 YARDS

The eighth hole, par 4 and 467 yards.

the time he arrived in Pinehurst, in 1900, and completed 18 holes in 1907. Even though he laid sand greens, his design work drew attention. By 1910 he had so many requests he gave up his summertime job at the Oakley Country Club near Boston, settled permanently in Pinehurst and developed into the premier designer of American golf courses.

Ross died in 1948, feeling he had done all he could with No. 2. By then he had raised it to the game's highest levels. In the subsequent 57 years, the course he left behind had inspired players and architects as well. They marveled at its creative flair.

Tufts believed he knew the key. Writing 20 years after Ross's death, Tufts claimed Ross never would permit himself to design a golf hole that was not both natural and beautiful.

"There is a sense of balance and lack of artificiality about his work that few architects have ever matched," Tufts wrote. "He was himself a very fine golfer, and having been brought up in the old school where finesse and skill were highly appreciated, he designed his holes to develop these more subtle aspects of the game. And yet he never forgot that golf must be a pleasure and not a penance."

One of six children of a stonemason, Ross was born in 1873 in Dornoch, Scotland, a small town on the North Sea. Fascinated with the game as a boy, he apprenticed to a carpenter at 14, and at 18 moved to St. Andrews, where for two years he worked as a clubmaker in the Robert Forgan shop, one of the more famous of all the early club-making factories.

Most important of all, he fell under the spell of Old Tom Morris, who had developed an exceptional ability in his own design work for following the ground's natural flow. With Morris's guidance, Ross studied the quirks of the Old

11th
PAR 4
476 YARDS

Course and worked its sweeps and sudden elevation changes into his designs. Simulating elements of the immense double greens at St. Andrews, he learned to create a big green that at the same time presents a small target. Early in the 1920s, in the midst of building Oak Hill in Rochester, he met 18-year-old Robert Trent Jones, who even then showed a keen interest in golf course design.

"Always remember, Laddie," Ross told him, "the green is the heart of the hole," and every effort should be made to situate it in the most natural position.

Looking back on those days at Oak Hill, Jones said, "Taken as a whole, they were an ingenious mix of crowns, hogbacks, terraces and slopes that forced the golfer to use his intelligence."

The greens in the early years of Pinehurst's restoration were different from those we know today. Ross certainly planned greens that would reject something less than a good shot, but over time his gentle slopes and grades grew more severe as green speeds increased.

The hallmark of a Ross course reaches beyond its greens, though. Some time ago Pete Dye, one of the premier architects of our time, named Ross one of the few architects who put a purpose behind each shot.

"His strategy was really simple. He was the first to balance out a golf course. I was stationed in North Carolina during the Second World War

12th
PAR 4
449 YARDS

and played No. 2 a lot. I noticed that Ross would have the main hazard on one side of one green and on the other side of the next. He'd make the good player feel ill at ease on the tee because he'd be asked to play one hole left to right and the next hole just the opposite."

Tom Fazio, another of our best at the craft, believes no first-class architect could help being influenced by Ross, if only for his belief that Ross created the best routing plans ever done. He feels that No. 2 stands out.

"His shot values are tremendous; if you look at the first and second holes at No. 2 you'll see there's not much ground movement, no severe changes of eleva-

13th
PAR 4
378 YARDS

The 13th hole, par 4 and 378 yards.

The 16th hole, par 4 and 492 yards.

14th
PAR 4
468 YARDS

482 yards, the last segment uphill to a canted green. Few holes play as tough as the fifth. The 1999 Open field averaged 4.54 strokes. Taking pity, the USGA scaled it back to 472 yards in 2005. The 2005 field averaged 4.395 shots.

Nevertheless, the 2005 Open field played a course that, at 7,214 yards, measured 92 yards longer than in 1999, even though a comparison of scorecards shows just a 39-yard difference. Unfortunately, the 1999 measurements were off by 53 yards.

tions, but he created dramatic angles into the greens."

Ross had tinkered with No. 2 almost from the time he finished the original design, but he went beyond dabbling by his complete rebuilding process in the middle 1930s. Using mules and drag pans, he reshaped each of the greens as he converted them to bermudagrass, along the way eliminating some weak holes and adding the current fourth and fifth holes, the fourth a shortish par 5 and the fifth a long par 4 of

15th
PAR 3
203 YARDS

16th
PAR 4
492 YARDS

Like Ross, the USGA did some tinkering as well. Because the greens of the eighth and 16th, both normally par 5s, can be reached with the second shot, they played as par 4s, the eighth at 467 yards and the 16th at 492 yards, three yards longer than in 1999. Seven new tees went into play, fairways were tightened to 25 to 28 yards, roughly three to four yards narrower than in 1999, and the rough was cut to three inches, short enough for players to get their clubs on the ball but deep enough to challenge their control. Throughout the week, the USGA tried for green speeds between 11 to 11.5 inches on the Stimpmeter.

Otherwise, aside from added length, little has changed over the last half century. With just a few exceptions, the holes run along fairly level ground, weaving through woodlands mostly of pine but with scattered white dogwood and old magnolias, maples and other hardwoods, so dense each hole seems isolated from civilization.

The fourth hole plays from a high tee to a valley below, and the fifth plays back to the high ground. In lengthening No. 2, the first tee, once nothing more than a level patch of ground, has been pushed back and slightly elevated, but the green, sitting some 400 yards away, is still hard to distinguish without the flag waffling in a gentle breeze.

The course begins to show its distance quickly, with the par-4 second a demanding 469 yards, but then the challenge turns to finesse with the 336-yard third, the No. 2's shortest par 4. Still, it is no pushover. Sam Snead called it the best short par 4 in the game. Here the best tee shot hugs the left side of the fairway, where Ross set a pair of bunkers, opening a shot to a green guarded by three more bunkers. The 2005 field averaged 4.069 strokes, but Michael Campbell played it in even par, Tiger Woods in two over par, and Retief Goosen played the third in one over par.

Once again the fourth, one of only two par 5s, gave up 193 birdies in 1999 and 155 in 2005, more than any other hole. The 10th, the other par 5, has been another matter. It surrendered just 52 birdies six years earlier and 88 in the latest Open.

It was on this hole that Ben Hogan played one of the more memorable shots in any Ryder Cup.

17th PAR 3 190 YARDS

18th PAR 4 442 YARDS

One up against Charley Ward after 27 holes of the singles, Hogan hooked his drive into the pines, giving Ward hope, then punched a low shot out to the fairway and ripped into a wooden club. The ball ran onto the green, he holed from 60 feet for a birdie 4, and he won the match, 3 and 2.

The 10th had been stretched out to 607 yards for the Open, the beginning of a stern stretch of holes measuring 476, 449, a breather at 378 and 468 yards leading up to the climactic closing holes, the holes that will be remembered for Stewart's resolve. Even with Mickelson and Woods after his 15th hole, he missed the 16th green, but he holed from 25 feet to save par and birdied the 17th, a par 3, moving one stroke in front. After pushing his drive into the woods right of the 18th fairway, he chopped out, pitched to 15 feet, then holed his putt for the par and beat Mickelson by a stroke.

No. 2 is, of course, a wonderful test of golf, but Pinehurst projects a distinct atmosphere. Those who play there often feel an affection for No. 2 unlike their reaction to other courses. They respect Pebble Beach, Cypress Point, Pine Valley and Augusta, but it isn't the same as for Pinehurst. Maybe it's because they sensed Pinehurst belonged to those who played there, or, perhaps, because Pinehurst welcomed them for nothing more than their enjoyment of the game.

The 18th hole, par 4 and 442 yards.

Bernhard Langer earned a place in sectional qualifying for his 20th U.S. Open Championship.

105th U.S. OPEN Qualifying

While it is true that anyone may enter the U.S. Open Championship, a high portion of those entered must go through a series of qualifying trials to earn places in the starting field. It is equally true that talented foreign golfers often are reluctant to spend the time and money on the off chance of surviving one day of qualifying.

As a remedy, the USGA established two qualifying sites in foreign countries, one in Ono City, Japan, about 50 miles south of Osaka, and the other at Walton Heath, near London.

Without this innovation, Michael Campbell would not have won the 2005 championship. After accepting the trophy, he said quite candidly that without it he would not have entered.

Campbell qualified with eight others at Walton Heath and three qualified in Japan.

Qualifiers made up the bulk of the starting field of 156 by winning 84 of the places. Based on their playing records, another 72 were fully exempt.

All told, a record 9,048 players filed entries and, of those, 8,758 had to play in one of 107 local qualifying rounds to select the 550 who would advance to the second step. Then they joined another 294 in 16 sectional tests over 36 holes to make up the starting field. The 2005 Open would not have been the same without them.

Olin Browne, for example, played his sectional rounds at Woodmont Country Club, in the Maryland suburbs of Washington, and nearly walked off in disgust after an opening 73. Assuming he had lost any hope of reaching Pinehurst, he asked the proper way to withdraw.

Fortunately Browne changed his mind, began his second round with an outward 30, came back in 29, shot 59, and at 132 qualified with strokes to spare. In a stunning finish, he birdied the 16th, holed a 110-yard pitch and eagled the 17th, reached the green of the 18th, a par 5, with his second shot and holed from 30 feet for a second eagle, picking up five strokes in three holes.

Rocco Mediate qualified at Woodmont as well, along with Matt Every, the Open's low amateur. Browne and Mediate shot 67 and led the first round, although neither held on to the end.

Nor could Jason Gore, perhaps the most surprising of all. After shooting 66-67–133 at East Lake, in Atlanta, Gore played such strong golf through the first three rounds he won a place in the last pairing of the fourth round, alongside Retief Goosen, the 54-hole leader.

Meantime, Bernhard Langer earned a place in his 20th Open by shooting 67-67–134 over two courses in Columbus, Ohio. While Langer has won two Masters Tournaments, he had placed as high as fourth in only one Open, and in 19 previous appearances he had survived the 36-hole cut in just nine. Qualifying with him, Australian Geoff Ogilvy led the field with 131. At the same time, Joe Ogilvie, an American, qualified, along with Bob Tway, a former PGA champion.

Tom Kite, the 1992 champion, ended his string of 32 consecutive Opens by shooting 140 at Woodmont, five strokes too many. Jose Maria Olazabal missed, as well as Brad Faxon, Jesper Parnevik and Jeff Sluman, who had played well earlier.

And Nick Faldo, who played his way into the field in 2004, didn't bother to try.

Players Who Were Fully Exempt for the 2005 U.S. Open (73)

Robert Allenby	8	Retief Goosen	1, 8, 9, 10, 12, 13, 16	Jeff Maggert	8
Stephen Ames	8, 9, 16			Shigeki Maruyama	8, 9, 16
Stuart Appleby	9, 16	Richard Green	15	Shaun Micheel	5
Rich Beem	5	Jay Haas	8, 9, 16	Phil Mickelson	3, 8, 9, 11, 12, 16
Thomas Bjorn	16	Todd Hamilton	4, 9, 16		
Bart Bryant	12	Padraig Harrington	10, 16	Colin Montgomerie	16
Angel Cabrera	10, 16	Mark Hensby	9, 16	Ryan Moore	2
Chad Campbell	9, 16	Tim Herron	8, 16	Nick O'Hern	10, 16
Paul Casey	10	Charles Howell III	16	Rod Pampling	16
K.J. Choi	9, 16	David Howell	10, 13, 16	Craig Parry	16
Stewart Cink	9, 16	Peter Jacobsen	7	Corey Pavin	1
Tim Clark	8, 16	Lee Janzen	1	Kenny Perry	9, 11, 12, 16
Darren Clarke*	9, 10, 16	Miguel Angel Jimenez	10, 16	Ian Poulter	10, 16
Fred Couples	16	Zach Johnson	9, 16	Nick Price	17
Ben Curtis	4	Steve Jones	1	Rory Sabbatini	9, 16
John Daly	9, 16	Shingo Katayama	14	Adam Scott	9, 11, 16
Chris DiMarco	8, 9, 11, 16	Jerry Kelly	9, 16	Vijay Singh	5, 9, 11, 12, 16
Luke Donald	11, 16	Tom Lehman	16	Toru Taniguchi	14
David Duval	4	Justin Leonard	11, 12, 16	David Toms	5, 9, 11, 16
Ernie Els	1, 4, 8, 9, 10, 12, 16	Thomas Levet	10	Scott Verplank	9, 16
Steve Flesch	8, 9	Spencer Levin	8	Mike Weir	3, 8, 9, 16
Carlos Franco	9	Luke List	2	Lee Westwood	10, 16
Fred Funk	6, 8, 9, 16	Peter Lonard	16	Tiger Woods	1, 3, 4, 5, 9, 11, 12, 16
Jim Furyk	1, 8, 11, 16	Davis Love III	9, 16		
Stephen Gallacher	10	Graeme McDowell	10, 16	*Withdrew; replaced by qualifying alternate Conrad Ray	
Sergio Garcia	9, 10, 12, 16	Paul McGinley	16		

Key to Player Exemptions:

1. Winners of the U.S. Open Championship for the last 10 years.
2. Winner and runner-up of the 2004 U.S. Amateur Championship.
3. Winners of the Masters Tournament the last five years.
4. Winners of the British Open Championship the last five years.
5. Winners of the PGA of America Championship the last five years.
6. Winner of the 2005 Players Championship.
7. Winner of the 2004 U.S. Senior Open Championship.
8. From the 2004 U.S. Open Championship, the 15 lowest scorers and anyone tying for 15th place.
9. From the 2004 final official PGA Tour money list, the top 30 money leaders.
10. From the 2004 final official PGA European Tour, the top 15 money leaders.
11. From the 2005 official PGA Tour money list, the top 10 money leaders through May 30.
12. Any multiple winner of PGA Tour co-sponsored events whose victories are considered official from April 22, 2004 through June 7, 2005.
13. From the 2005 PGA European Tour, the top two money leaders through May 31.
14. From the 2004 final Japan Golf Tour money list, the top two leaders provided they are within the top 75 point leaders of the World Rankings at that time.
15. From the 2004 final PGA Tour of Australasia money list, the top two leaders provided they are within the top 75 point leaders of the World Rankings at that time.
16. From the World Rankings list, the top 50 point leaders as of May 31.
17. Special exemptions selected by the USGA Executive Committee. International players not otherwise exempt as selected by the USGA Executive Committee.

Sectional Qualifying Results

Ono Golf Club
Ono City, Hyogo, Japan
17 players for 3 spots
Steven Conran, Australia, 69-67–136
Yong Eun Yang, Korea, 68-70–138
(P)Keiichiro Fukabori, Japan, 71-69–140

El Caballero Country Club
Tarzana, Calif.
68 players for 4 spots
Nick Jones, Los Angeles, Calif., 67-72–139
(P)Scott Gibson, Huntington Beach, Calif., 73-67–140
(P)Michael Ruiz, Las Vegas, Nev., 72-68–140
(P)Eric Meichtry, Murrieta, Calif., 70-70–140
**Conrad Ray, Palo Alto, Calif., 71-69–140

Columbine Country Club
Littleton, Colo.
28 players for 1 spot
Wil Collins, Rapid City, S.D., 71-70–141

Walton Heath Golf Club
Surrey, England
53 players for 9 spots
Peter Hanson, Sweden, 66-68–134
Jonathan Lomas, England, 68-66–134
Simon Dyson, England, 67-70–137
Soren Kjeldsen, Denmark, 69-69–138
Michael Campbell, New Zealand, 68-71–139
Robert Karlsson, Sweden, 70-69–139
Nick Dougherty, England, 73-66–139
Jose-Filipe Lima, Portugal, 71-68–139
Peter Hedblom, Sweden, 74-65–139

East Lake Golf Club
Atlanta, Ga.
77 players for 6 spots
Derek Brown, Walnut Cove, N.C., 65-66–131
Jason Gore, Valencia, Calif., 66-67–133
Casey Wittenberg, Memphis, Tenn., 66-67–133
Aaron Barber, Maple Grove, Minn., 66-68–134
Scott Parel, Augusta, Ga., 69-65–134
(P)Matt Kuchar, Atlanta, Ga., 69-66–135

Michael Campbell

Bob Estes

Olin Browne

Qualifying

Kaanapali Golf Club
Lahaina, Hawaii
12 players for 1 spot
*Pierre-Henri Soero, New Caledonia, 70-77–147

Village Links of Glen Ellyn
Glen Ellyn, Ill.
30 players for 2 spots
Jerry Smith, Scottsdale, Ariz., 70-68–138
James Benepe, Sheridan, Wyo., 69-71–140

Woodmont Country Club
Rockville, Md.
156 players for 22 spots
J.P. Hayes, El Paso, Texas, 62-67–129
Tommy Armour III, Las Colinas, Texas, 68-63–131
*David Denham, Tifton, Ga., 64-67–131
Olin Browne, Hobe Sound, Fla., 73-59–132
Craig Barlow, Henderson, Nev., 67-66–133
James Driscoll, Jupiter, Fla., 66-67–133
Clint Jensen, Palm Beach Gardens, Fla., 69-64–133
Rocco Mediate, Naples, Fla., 65-68–133
Rob Rashell, Everett, Wash., 65-68–133
Brandt Snedeker, Nashville, Tenn., 66-67–133
Omar Uresti, Austin, Texas, 64-69–133
D.J. Brigman, Albuquerque, N.M., 68-66–134
Steve Elkington, Houston, Texas, 67-67–134
Ryuji Imada, Tampa, Fla., 66-68–134
John Mallinger, Escondido, Calif., 67-67–134
David Oh, Cerritos, Calif., 67-67–134
*Lee Williams, Alexander City, Ala., 67-67–134
*(P)Michael Putnam, University Place, Wash., 69-66–135
(P)Ian Leggatt, Canada, 67-68–135
(P)David Hearn, Canada, 68-67–135
(P)Franklin Langham, Peachtree City, Ga., 68-67–135
*(P)Matt Every, Daytona Beach, Fla., 69-66–135

Chevy Chase Country Club
Rockville, Md.
16 players for 1 spot
Paul Claxton, Claxton, Ga., 66-66–132

Canoe Brook Country Club
Summit, N.J.
84 players for 6 spots
Michael Allen, Scottsdale, Ariz., 68-68–136
Chris Nallen, Scottsdale, Ariz., 70-68–138
J.L. Lewis, Lakeway, Texas, 70-68–138
Len Mattiace, Jacksonville, Fla., 68-70–138
J.J. Henry, Ft. Worth, Texas, 68-71–139
Steve Allan, Scottsdale, Ariz., 67-73–140

Double Eagle Golf Club
Columbus, Ohio
17 players for 1 spot
(P)Patrick Damron, Orlando, Fla., 68-69–137

Steve Elkington

Nick Dougherty

Geoff Ogilvy

Robert Gamez

Brookside Golf and Country Club & Lakes Golf and Country Club
Columbus, Ohio
144 players for 20 spots
Geoff Ogilvy, Scottsdale, Ariz., 67-64–131
John Rollins, Richmond, Va., 67-66–133
Scott McCarron, Reno, Nev., 68-65–133
Bernhard Langer, Boca Raton, Fla., 67-67–134
John Cook, Orlando, Fla., 66-69–135
Arron Oberholser, Scottsdale, Ariz., 64-72–136
Bill Glasson, Stillwater, Okla., 68-68–136
Bob Tway, Edmond, Okla., 66-70–136
Carl Pettersson, Chapel Hill, N.C., 69-67–136
Euan Walters, Chattanooga, Tenn., 68-68–136
Joe Ogilvie, Austin, Texas, 67-69–136
John Merrick, Long Beach, Calif., 67-69–136
Robert Gamez, Celebration, Fla., 68-68–136
Ted Purdy, Phoenix, Ariz., 69-67–136
(P)Bob Estes, Austin, Texas, 71-66–137
(P)Brandt Jobe, Menlo Park, Calif., 68-69–137
(P)Eric Axley, Knoxville, Tenn., 66-71–137
(P)Frank Lickliter II, Ponte Vedra Beach, Fla., 69-68–137
(P)Sal Spallone, Vero Beach, Fla., 69-68–137
(P)Steve Lowery, Birmingham, Ala., 66-71–137

Rocco Mediate

TPC at Craig Ranch
McKinney, Texas
34 players for 2 spots
*Trip Kuehne, Irving, Texas, 68-68–136
(P)Kyle Willmann, Oklahoma City, Okla., 71-67–138

TPC at Snoqualmie Ridge
Snoqualmie, Wash.
17 players for 1 spot
Troy Kelly, Bremerton, Wash., 70-68–138

Old Memorial Golf Club
Tampa, Fla.
52 players for 3 spots
Lee Rinker, Jupiter, Fla., 69-67–136
Nick Gilliam, Gainesville, Fla., 67-72–139
Josh McCumber, Gainesville, Fla., 69-70–139

Hallbrook Country Club
Kansas City, Mo.
26 players for 1 spot
Tom Pernice, Murrieta, Calif., 70-69–139

Brandt Jobe

Trip Kuehne

*Denotes amateur   (P) Won playoff
**Qualified when exempt player Darren Clarke withdrew

When Olin Browne teed off, he didn't attract much notice, but several hours later he had 67 and everyone's attention.

105th U.S. OPEN
First Round

Six years earlier, in 1999, when the USGA introduced Pinehurst No. 2 to the U.S. Open Championship, those who cared assumed this storied old course would play firm and fast from the beginning, sending scores to unaccustomed high figures. Instead, rain softened the ground, No. 2 became mildly yielding and 23 men broke its par of 70.

How times change.

On the Open's second visit, in June 2005, the weather remained dry, the ground remained firm, the sun blazed down and just nine men broke par.

Nevertheless, the field of 156 competitors could hardly have expected better playing conditions. Not that No. 2 had become benign — that can never be true — but as the first round opened, the wind, a slight breeze really, had little effect on ball flight, the fairways could hardly have been in better condition, and the greens, expected to resemble marble, held the well-played shot.

After playing a few holes, most players sensed the greens putted a bit slower than the advertised 11 to 11.5 Stimpmeter speed, perhaps because the USGA decided not to double-cut, a common procedure in championship golf.

Whatever the reason, the upper echelon of the first-round results included Olin Browne, Rocco Mediate, Brandt Jobe and Steve Jones, who had been among the missing since winning the 1996 Open. Of course, Retief Goosen stood among them as well, along with Phil Mickelson, Tiger Woods, Vijay Singh and Ernie Els, the entire top five of the world golf rankings. The leaders also included other respected players such as Lee Westwood, K.J. Choi, Luke Donald, David Toms and Adam Scott.

Mediate, whose chronic back problems drove him from the Tour for a time, shot 67, three strokes under Pinehurst's par, and matched Browne, who had considered dropping out of sectional qualifying because he believed he would have to shoot 62 in the second of the two rounds to have any chance of moving on to the U.S. Open. Instead he shot 59, and now he shared the lead with Mediate, who had qualified with him.

Behind them, Goosen, the 2001 and 2004 champion, shot 68 along with Jobe and Westwood, and one stroke further behind, at 69, came Mickelson, Donald, Choi and Jones, whose elbow problems had kept him away from tournament golf for a year or more.

Starting from the 10th tee, Woods ground out a respectable round of 70, the same score as Singh, and Els opened with 71.

A blistering hot sun had scorched Pinehurst early in the week. Temperatures on Wednesday, the day before the Open began, climbed into the mid-90s, but smothering humidity drove the heat index above 100. Only the occasional light breeze and the promise of cooler days ahead made it bearable. Nevertheless, temperatures approached 90 during the first round.

Whether the heat had an effect on how the course played could be debated, but obviously No. 2 had become quite difficult. Shots into those turtle-back greens that had been controllable in 1999 had turned to guesswork; the ball might roll anywhere — over the back, off the sides or even back down the slope to the golfer's feet.

Bill Glasson (74) had the honor of first off at 7 a.m.

To demonstrate, take the case of Stuart Appleby at the third hole, just 336 yards, Pinehurst's shortest par 4. Playing with Jobe and Japanese golfer Toru Taniguchi, Appleby had made his figures at the first two holes, but his approach to the third carried too far and ran off the back of the green and down a slope. His recovery, a high pitch, once again rolled off and disappeared into a bunker. Three strokes later he finally reached the green — his sixth shot — and with two putts he scored an 8. He shot 81 and lost all hope of playing over the weekend.

Lee Janzen had a similar experience, although not as costly, at the fifth hole, another of Pinehurst's difficult par 4s. From the left bunker so deep below the green he couldn't be seen, Janzen flew his recovery off the back, but, unlike Appleby, Janzen salvaged a bogey 5.

Now neither Janzen nor Appleby were hackers; Janzen had won the U.S. Open twice and Appleby brought an acceptable record with him. He had

Brandt Jobe (68) was four under par until taking a bogey here at the 16th hole and another at the 17th.

First Round

Olin Browne	67	-3
Rocco Mediate	67	-3
Retief Goosen	68	-2
Lee Westwood	68	-2
Brandt Jobe	68	-2
Steve Jones	69	-1
Luke Donald	69	-1
K.J. Choi	69	-1
Phil Mickelson	69	-1
David Toms	70	E
Tiger Woods	70	E
Tommy Armour III	70	E
Adam Scott	70	E
Vijay Singh	70	E
Toru Taniguchi	70	E
Bob Estes	70	E

won the Mercedes Championships two years running and the week before the Open had tied for seventh in the Booz Allen Classic at Congressional Country Club, in Maryland, the site of the 1964 and 1997 Opens.

But the Open is different.

Still, any golf course can be beaten. Jones and Jobe both birdied four of the first six holes, and Browne scored five consecutive 3s on the second nine.

Playing in the second group off the first tee just after 7 a.m., Browne scraped out a par at the first hole, dropped a stroke at the second, then picked it up with a birdie at the fourth, a 565-yard par 5 that became No. 2's most vulnerable hole, the only hole with an average score lower than par over the four rounds.

Browne lost another stroke at the sixth, a testing 220-yard par 3 with a tempting false front. His ball didn't make the crest of the slope, rolled into a hollow, and he missed a 12-foot putt. Once again, though, he made up for it by birdieing the ninth, the softest of the four par 3s, with a stunning 6-iron to about two feet. Out in 35, even par, he started back with three routine pars before his streak of five 3s.

Retief Goosen (68) was smiling at the 13th after a birdie.

Lee Westwood (68) saved par at the 18th hole.

Right-leaning Rocco Mediate (67) followed his chip shot that led to a saving par 3 at the 15th hole.

This tee shot helped K.J. Choi (69) birdie the 10th.

From off the 13th green Browne holed a 20-foot putt for a birdie 3, and after playing a conservative approach to the 14th, a tough par 4, holed from 20 feet for another birdie. He followed with a par 3 at the equally tough 15th, then played perhaps his best shot of the day. From over 220 yards out and his ball in the rough, he tore into a 7-wood shot that ran onto the 16th green. He holed from 15 feet and birdied a hole that surrendered only 22 birdies throughout the four rounds. With pars at the 17th and 18th, Browne had come back in 32 and stood atop the leaderboard.

Mediate, meanwhile, played as steady a round as reasonable under the tension of an Open championship. He strayed from par on only four holes, just one for a bogey at the 14th, which claimed 60 bogeys that day. Only the fifth, 15th and 16th took more.

Out in 34 with a birdie at the fourth from four feet, Mediate played a Promethean drive at the 607-yard 10th, the longest hole in an Open since the 642-yard fifth at Southern Hills in 2001. From

Steve Jones (69) had just two pars on the first nine.

Luke Donald (69) took 28 putts in his first round.

about 260 yards, Mediate ripped into a 3-wood shot that rolled within 50 feet of the hole. He holed it, of course, for an eagle 3. It had to be the shot of the day, and it dropped him to three under par. A lost stroke at the 14th, where he thinned a 9-iron and flew his ball over the green, and a 6-iron to about eight feet for another tough birdie at the 16th, and Mediate had his 67. Now he and Browne would have to wait for the rest of the field to finish.

Both men were unlikely leaders. Browne, of course, had been perhaps five minutes away from withdrawing, but he had nearly walked away from tournament golf in the winter of 2004. He had struggled on the Tour for a few years and had lost his exempt status. He felt himself wearing down physically as well.

Not ready to give up entirely, he had surgery on his elbow and, after help from a teaching guru, regained his game. Although not one of the more dangerous players in professional golf, he'd had a decent record. He had won at both the Colonial, in Fort Worth, and at Hartford in the late 1990s, and had tied for fifth in the 1997 U.S. Open, at Congressional. Now, at the age of 46, he had a shot at the Open once again.

Mediate had gone through pain and suffering as well, especially from a back problem. Once a steady money winner, he had made only 13 cuts over the last two seasons, with good reason. As he bent over a trophy case in his home in March 2004, Mediate's back locked. Not able to move, he hung on for three hours, then somehow crawled up a flight of stairs to his bed. Speaking about his condition after the first round, he said his back pain had finally eased about a month before the Open. Since the incident, though, he had lost about 25 pounds and rebuilt his swing to relieve pressure on his back. Apparently it worked. And so did his change from a belly putter to the more conventional club.

Jones had missed two years of tournament golf because of a balky elbow and wondered if he would ever play again. He was told he needed surgical repair on a tendon, had the operation in August

Phil Mickelson (69) said the greens were 'very fair.'

Tiger Woods (70) drove in the 16th rough and bogeyed.

2003 and began the long trip back. Now he found himself in the thick of the Open once again, two strokes off the lead.

Playing with Bob Tway and David Duval, immediately ahead of Mediate, Jones parred only the fifth and eighth holes on the outward nine, yet shot 34. He birdied four holes and bogeyed three, but played a more steady second nine.

Jones began by birdieing the first with a pitch to five feet, drove into the rough at the second, bunkered his approach and missed from six feet, then lofted a sand wedge to 15 feet and birdied the third. Two under par now, he added another birdie at the fourth with a precise pitch inside 10 feet, then he played what he called his best shot of the day. From the tee of the sixth, he spanked a 3-iron that hit the upward slope of the false front and died less than 10 feet from the hole. He holed for his fourth birdie.

Three bogeys brought Jones back to even par, but he picked up one more stroke at the 13th with another flawless pitch to two feet, shot 69, and at the end of the day tied Donald, Mickelson and Choi.

Jones admitted he had missed playing the past few years, and said, "Yes, I missed playing, period. You just try to be ready, and when it's your turn, you try to make the most of it."

Goosen, meanwhile, played the kind of steady round necessary to win at this level. Driving long and straight — he averaged 305 yards at the two measured holes — and playing first-class irons, he cruised around No. 2 in 68 strokes, a score that, in truth, deserved to be a few strokes lower with better putting. He missed only the fifth, 10th and 16th fairways and the first and 16th greens. He birdied the fourth, 10th and 13th holes, and bogeyed only the 14th, where he three-putted.

At about the same time Goosen began his round from the first tee, just before 8 a.m., Tiger Woods teed off at the 10th and immediately slashed a drive right of the fairway and onto a dirt path. No problem. He scowled, then played a nice shot within easy range of the green, pitched on within 10 feet of the hole and holed for a birdie 4.

Two holes later, playing the 12th, an out-

Ernie Els (71) hit five fairways.   *Bob Estes (70) started poorly.*   *Vijay Singh (70) wasn't happy.*

standing par 4 with wiregrass lining the right side, Woods pushed his third consecutive drive and landed among the grasses. Using a 3-wood, he ran his ball within 10 feet of the hole again, but missed the birdie putt. Clearly he wasn't playing as he had three years earlier, when he won at Bethpage.

After scraping out pars at the 11th and 14th, Woods was short of the green with his tee shot to the 15th, another dangerous par 3, and lost a stroke, and right away lost another at the 16th, the 492-yard par 4 that normally plays as a par 5. It was here that an overeager photographer snapped a picture with Woods in the middle of his backswing. After a few choice words, Woods missed the green and took his punishment, then closed out the nine with routine pars at the last two holes. He had played the second nine in 36, one over par.

Moving on to the first nine, he played the first two holes in par, saving his 4 at the second with one putt. After waiting about five minutes for the group ahead to clear the third green, Woods, trying to play a low fade short of the right greenside bunker, pushed his drive so far right it looked as if he was taking a shortcut to the sixth tee, which runs parallel. Before it got there, it slammed against a tall pine tree and ricocheted to the right of that bunker. Mission accomplished, although not as planned.

Obviously Woods and his driver weren't getting along, but he still made his par, then moved on to the fourth, where he drove into the rough once more, followed with a 6-iron into a greenside bunker, pitched out within a foot of the hole and made his second birdie of the round. Back to even par, he played the remainder of the holes in even par and finished with a round of 70.

Just three strokes off the lead with 54 holes to play, Woods remained the most dangerous man in the field.

Jason Gore (138) won over the spectators with his demeanor, and with 67 in the second round, shared the lead.

As the U.S. Open advanced through the second round, strange things happened. Retief Goosen climbed into a first-place tie, which wasn't at all unexpected, but those alongside him certainly surprised the galleries. Goosen shot 70 his second time around Pinehurst's demanding No. 2 course, two strokes above his opening round, yet still climbed upward, and there beside him stood Olin Browne, who held onto a share of first, and Jason Gore, a bulky 31-year-old Californian who had struggled on the Nationwide Tour, a farm system for the PGA Tour.

Browne added 71 to his opening 67, and Gore shot 67 after an opening 71. All three had 138, two under par, for the 36 holes.

Meanwhile, over a stretch of seven holes, Rocco Mediate bogeyed five, shot 74 and dropped into a tie for 10th at 141. Seven others matched 141, among them Tiger Woods, still hanging around within three strokes of the lead.

In other developments:

Peter Hedblom raced around No. 2 in 66 strokes, not only the lowest score of the week, but 11 strokes better than his first round as well.

David Toms, in position to take the lead, played his last two holes in five over par and fell into a 17th-place tie with two others, at 142.

Chris DiMarco, who nearly won the Masters Tournament in April, shot 82 and missed the 36-hole cut. Phil Mickelson, two strokes out of first place after the first round, shot 77 and, with 146, dropped like a rock into a tie for 45th. Also from the world's top-five ranked players, Ernie Els was a stroke further back, tied for 57th, at 147, after his 76.

And Michael Campbell announced his presence with 69 and 140.

Ahead of Campbell, in fourth place at 139, were K.J. Choi and Mark Hensby. Sharing sixth place at 140 with Campbell were Vijay Singh, Sergio Garcia and Lee Westwood. There was the 10th-place group at 141 that included Woods and Mediate.

Then there was Corey Pavin, the 1995 Open champion.

Pavin had a schedule problem. His son was to graduate from high school the night of the Open's first round, and Pavin wanted to be in two places at once. Consequently, he had a 7:22 a.m. starting time on Thursday and a 12:32 p.m. time for Friday. His first round over, Pavin rushed to the Moore County airport, boarded a private plane, flew to San Diego and attended the graduation, rushed back to the airport and returned early enough to take a short nap and meet his Friday time. Pavin shot 73-72–145 and tied for 33rd.

A slight overcast hung over Pinehurst as the second round began, and the temperature fell slightly to the low 80s, a level more comfortable for the galleries. Spectators had poured through the gates in great numbers, estimated at about 38,000 each day. They crowded against the restraining ropes lining the holes, some following a particular player or group, while others found a spot with a view and camped out for the day.

Sadists settled on camp chairs under shade trees near the green of the fifth, a very tough par 4 where pars were precious and bogeys common. From there they could watch every shot from tee to green.

Most spectators, though, took the more posi-

Second Round

Retief Goosen (138) shot 70 despite three bogeys.

Second Round

Olin Browne	67 – 71	– 138	-2
Retief Goosen	68 – 70	– 138	-2
Jason Gore	71 – 67	– 138	-2
K.J. Choi	69 – 70	– 139	-1
Mark Hensby	71 – 68	– 139	-1
Michael Campbell	71 – 69	– 140	E
Vijay Singh	70 – 70	– 140	E
Sergio Garcia	71 – 69	– 140	E
Lee Westwood	68 – 72	– 140	E
Adam Scott	70 – 71	– 141	+1
Jim Furyk	71 – 70	– 141	+1
Brandt Jobe	68 – 73	– 141	+1
Tiger Woods	70 – 71	– 141	+1
Rocco Mediate	67 – 74	– 141	+1
Steve Allan	72 - 69	– 141	+1
Keiichiro Fukabori	74 – 67	– 141	+1

tive view and sought out players who scored well. If they arrived early enough they might have caught Hedblom, a 35-year-old Swede with spiky blond hair sticking above his blue visor and wearing a peach-colored shirt and blue trousers. Hedblom would rather play ice hockey, though, but broke his leg in a game late in 2001 and missed the 2002 golf season. Golf being the more survivable game, Hedblom returned to it in 2003, and now qualified at Walton Heath for his first U.S. Open.

There was one hitch. Somewhere between Stockholm and Newark, N.J., his port of entry, the airline misplaced his clubs. He arrived at Pinehurst Saturday evening, borrowed a sand wedge and a putter Sunday morning and walked the course, playing little pitches into the greens and testing his putting stroke, and spent much of Monday fretting about his clubs.

They arrived Tuesday, minutes before his scheduled practice round, which he had intended to play with borrowed clubs, but at least he had his familiar equipment, although it didn't seem to have helped much at first. He played a shaky 77 in the first round, running off eight bogeys and a single birdie, but suddenly he found his game the next day and played an inspiring round of 66. In the first

Olin Browne (138) took 5 at the par-3 sixth.

group off, at 7 a.m., Hedblom opened with a birdie and never let up.

Beginning from the first tee, Hedblom split the fairway with his drive, followed with a pitching wedge to six feet and holed the putt for an opening 3. He picked up another birdie at the fourth with a pitch from a greenside bunker to six feet once again, then added another at the eighth, the converted par 5. A 3-wood and 7-iron left him a putt of 40 feet or more, and he ran it in for the 3.

Out in 32, he played the 607-yard 10th with a drive into the right rough, an 8-iron out and a 7-iron to about 40 feet, and again holed the putt. Four under now, he lost a stroke at the 14th where he missed a three-foot putt for the par.

He had played a steady and, except for the missed three-footer, almost error-free round, hitting 10 of 14 fairways on driving holes, and although he missed seven greens, he putted like a dream.

At the same time, Goosen played not nearly as well as he had in the first round. Where he had hit 11 fairways and 16 greens, the next day he kept his ball on the fairway of just five holes and 10 greens. Of course, some of those missed fairways were a matter of a foot or so into the secondary rough, but the ball is more controllable from the short grass.

K.J. Choi (139) posted 70 with a birdie at the 18th.

Second Round

Mark Hensby (139) played the second nine in 33 for 68.

Michael Campbell (140) hit 11 of the 14 fairways.

He did begin with a birdie at the 10th, the first of five consecutive greens in regulation, but he missed the green of the 15th, a very difficult par 3 of 203 yards, and played the second nine — his first — in 35, even par.

Picking up the pace, Goosen dropped to two under par after four holes of his second nine, but he missed the green of the fifth and overshot the seventh, two par 4s, and fell back to even par. Still, he had climbed into a tie for first.

Browne had surprised everyone with his opening 67, but to find Jason Gore among the elite beggared belief. Except he had led the Open once before. Playing the first hole at Olympic in 1998, he holed a wedge, and for a brief moment stood at the top of the leaderboard. It didn't last, of course, but this time it was for real.

Gore leaves the distinct impression he enjoys what he does. Even after four-putting the fifth green for a double-bogey 6 in the opening round, he walked away smiling. His only comment: "What can you do? It's the U.S. Open. Things like that happen."

A sandy-haired, round-faced, 235-pound mass of good humor, Gore began the season playing wherever he could, mostly on the Nationwide Tour, but occasionally in local California tournaments. To reach the Open he fought through both local and sectional qualifying rounds, one of only 30 who made it, and then, on his way to Pinehurst, someone burgled his car. The thief stole his wife's clothes, but only his underwear and his computer. And his eight-month-old son had an ear infection.

Still, smiling all the way, Gore began his day from the 10th tee just before 2 p.m. and played four holes before he parred. He pitched to 10 feet and birdied the 10th, butchered the 11th and had to hole from 12 feet to save a bogey, came right back and birdied the 12th with a sand wedge to 20 feet, holed from inside 10 feet and birdied the 13th, then bogeyed the 15th.

With 34 on the second nine, he played the first in 33 with a birdie at the fourth and a rare 2 at the sixth following a beautifully played 4-iron to about 15 feet.

While Gore had played about as well as he

Adam Scott (141) had 71 with five bogeys.

could, Olin Browne slacked off from his first-round heroics. But even though he claimed he didn't play very well, he still turned in a quite respectable 71 and held onto a share of first place. It had been a struggle, though, helped along by 10 one-putt greens, among them a 20-footer to save a double bogey at the dangerous sixth.

Beginning from the 10th tee, Browne made the turn in 36 with a bogey at the 14th, where he avoided something worse by holing from eight feet. He dipped to one under par with birdies at the second and third, the second with a 5-iron from the rough to about 15 feet and the third with a putt of 20 feet when his approach ran past the flagstick.

Then the par-3 sixth. Played slightly off-line to the left, his tee shot dived into a bunker, his pitch carried over the green and into another bunker, then back over the green once again with his third. Lying 3, he played a timid chip that left him about 20 feet from the hole, then ran it in for a double-bogey 5. Speaking of it later, Browne said, "I got away with murder on that hole."

Pars in and he held on for his 71 and 138.

While Goosen, Browne and Gore led the championship, the biggest galleries still followed Woods, who hit the ball all over the county, yet kept himself in reach of the leaders, with 71 and 141. Yet he showed a touch of frustration toward the middle of his round.

Sergio Garcia (140) was frustrated by three short misses.

Jim Furyk (141) shot 70 but bogeyed his last two holes.

Second Round

Tiger Woods (141) bogeyed from the rough at the eighth.

David Toms (142) was three under after 34 holes.

Lee Westwood (140) shot 72 and was even par.

Playing from the first tee, Woods flew his drive into the right rough, then tugged at the right sleeve of his shirt. At first the gallery suspected he had strained a muscle, but he claimed a too tight sleeve had restricted his backswing. One hole later his caddie drew out a knife and sliced the seam. Problem solved.

Meantime, from that dense rough, Woods slashed a 9-iron onto the green and saved his par 4, followed with a solid drive at the 469-yard second, played a 9-iron to 15 feet and birdied. One under now. Right away he lost it when his approach to the third spun off the green, but then got another birdie at the fourth, where he reached the green with a blistering 3-iron and got down in two putts.

All the while Woods had struggled with his putting. Now, at the sixth, after a 5-iron to the front edge of the green, he ran his first putt 20 feet past the hole and bogeyed. Three holes later, at the ninth, another par 3, from 30 feet away he rolled his putt 12 feet past and missed once again.

Peter Hedblom (143) shot 66.   *Ernie Els (147) fell to 76.*   *Phil Mickelson (146) posted 77.*

Fuming, Woods then slashed against the green, scraped the grass and caused mild damage. He attempted to smooth it out, but it still showed. Informed of the incident, the USGA ruled it did not constitute a serious breach of golf etiquette.

With a birdie at the 16th, Woods played the second nine in 34, but he had bogeyed four holes on the first nine mainly through lax driving and irons that left him so far from the hole he had little chance of holing putts. He had 34 putts that day, far too many for this level of competition, and yet there he was within reach of the championship.

While the galleries focused on Woods and Goosen, Campbell made the most significant move of the day. By shooting 69, just one stroke under par, he climbed 11 places, from a tie for 17th into a tie for sixth. His could hardly be called a rock-steady round, though. He birdied six holes and bogeyed five, which meant he parred only seven.

A regular on the European Tour, Campbell is a Maori, descending from New Zealand's indigenous people. Thirty-six years old, he was known only by the most dedicated golf fans in the United States, although he had played in six previous Opens. And yet here he was among the leaders.

Off early, Campbell played steady golf from the tee, hitting 11 of the 14 fairways, but he missed six greens, a costly mistake at No. 2, and he three-putted twice, losing strokes at the 11th and 14th. But he saved pars by one-putting three holes, including the 18th, where he missed both the fairway and the green.

Nevertheless, he broke par by one stroke and climbed into contention. The next day he would be among the 83 survivors of the first two rounds, among the largest fields ever after the 36-hole cut. The cut fell at 148, a high figure, and caught, among others, Todd Hamilton, the 2004 British Open champion, Spencer Levin, the amateur who played the 17th hole at Shinnecock Hills the previous year in successive scores of 1, 2, 3 and 4, Scott Verplank, Padraig Harrington, Miguel Angel Jimenez, Chris DiMarco and David Duval, whose comeback was still pending.

After dropping three strokes at the 12th and 13th, Retief Goosen (207) was 'determined to have a better finish.'

Watching Retief Goosen amble three times around exacting Pinehurst No. 2 with all its quirks and still wear a monk-like expression of detached calm, a spectator crowded against the restraining ropes said to a friend, "The man's nerve ends must be numb."

A logical assumption considering how his third-round 69 broke his tie with Olin Browne and Jason Gore. Goosen took over first place alone and expanded his lead to three strokes with just 18 holes to play. Even when his situation had turned bleak after a bogey at the 12th and a double bogey at the 13th, Goosen's expression remained no expression at all. He simply birdied three of the last five holes, the toughest string of holes No. 2 had on offer, and moved into a position to win his third U.S. Open Championship.

Yet he had not shaken off Browne and Gore completely. Both men shot 72, two over par, and shared second place. Goosen led at 207 and Gore and Browne followed at 210, even par for three rounds. Michael Campbell was one stroke further behind at 211, tied for fourth with Mark Hensby, a 5-foot-8, 150-pound, 32-year-old Australian with an uninspiring record. But he tied for fifth place in the Masters earlier in the year.

Despite his poor finish, five over par at the eighth and ninth holes in the second round, David Toms played a steady round of 70, but at 212, five strokes behind and in sixth place, hardly seemed a threat. Nor did Tiger Woods, whose scores had climbed a stroke in each round, from 70, to 71, then 72. Woods shared seventh place at 213 with Peter Hedblom, Lee Westwood and K.J. Choi.

This had been a difficult day for everyone. The course had given up nine sub-par rounds the first day and 14 the second, yet only Goosen and 51-year-old Peter Jacobsen went as low as 69 in the third, just one stroke under the par of 70. Jacobsen relied on one shot.

Exempt from qualifying as the U.S. Senior Open champion, Jacobsen stepped onto the ninth tee one under par for the round and five over for the 36 holes. He estimated 174 yards to his target and played a 5-iron. The ball hit the front of the green, bounced once, then darted into the hole for a hole in one. The gallery roared and raised their arms like a football official signaling a touchdown.

"It was one of those shots that the minute it left the club I knew was fantastic," Jacobsen said.

Jacobsen beamed, went out in 32, followed up his ace with a birdie at the 10th, but then lost three strokes, came back in 37, and at 214 stood within seven strokes of Goosen.

While Jacobsen climbed up the leaderboard, other bright lights dimmed. Vijay Singh slipped to 74 after two rounds of 70, Phil Mickelson recovered somewhat from his 77 and shot 72, but at 218 remained out of touch with the leaders, and Ernie Els also shot 72, far behind at 219.

Accidental though it certainly was, the pairing of John Daly and Mickelson qualified as whimsical, Mickelson the straight-and-narrow All-American boy, Daly the mischievous loose cannon. He has, though, won the PGA Championship and the British Open, and Mickelson has won the 2004 Masters Tournament. Their followers reflected their personalities — Mickelson's dressed in golf shirts, Daly's wearing T-shirts. Still, it was an enlightening collision of opposite cultures.

Third Round

Phil Mickelson (218) was off very early.

Third Round

Retief Goosen	68 – 70 – 69 – 207	-3
Jason Gore	71 – 67 – 72 – 210	E
Olin Browne	67 – 71 – 72 – 210	E
Michael Campbell	71 – 69 – 71 – 211	+1
Mark Hensby	71 – 68 – 72 – 211	+1
David Toms	70 – 72 – 70 – 212	+2
Peter Hedblom	77 – 66 – 70 – 213	+3
Tiger Woods	70 – 71 – 72 – 213	+3
Lee Westwood	68 – 72 – 73 – 213	+3
K.J. Choi	69 – 70 – 74 – 213	+3
Peter Jacobsen	72 – 73 – 69 – 214	+4
Arron Oberholser	76 – 67 – 71 – 214	+4
Steve Allan	72 – 69 – 73 – 214	+4
Vijay Singh	70 – 70 – 74 – 214	+4

Aside from their mostly impeccable behavior, the size of the Pinehurst galleries surprised long-time Open observers. It had been standard with the USGA to schedule the championship close to metropolitan centers to attract large galleries. Pebble Beach in 1972 had been an exception, but San Francisco wasn't too far away and other cities lay close by. Shinnecock Hills and Bethpage, both on Long Island, could be reached with public transportation from New York. On the other hand, Pinehurst truly was remote.

Nevertheless, the fans came in great numbers, many to watch their favorites.

Other than Woods, Mickelson and Daly probably had the most devoted fans, but Jason Gore inspired his own following. It's easy to understand why. As Gore lumbered up the 18th fairway, waving his cap to the gallery, a stockily built spectator marveled, "He's me!"

Indeed, he had been called Everyman, and the fans adored him. Perhaps they felt a kinship because he smiles so easily, and, like them, pumps his own gas (he was spotted topping off his courtesy car) and runs errands for his family, such as a trip to the drugstore to pick up medication for his sick eight-month-old son. He can also play a little.

By the time Gore teed off, just before Goosen and Browne, Woods had been out for nearly an

Jason Gore (210) secured a place in Sunday's final pairing when he shot 72 with an 18-foot birdie putt at the last.

hour, struggling with his putter and growing more irritable with every stroke. With reason. Over the course of the third round, Woods hit 16 greens, which should have led to a bagful of birdies, but he made just one, at the 11th, the first of only two one-putt greens. They were balanced by two holes where he three-putted. With 36 putts, he counted more than any others high up in the standing.

That statistic does stand to reason, though. Since he reached so many greens, it is reasonable to consider that he had more opportunities to putt than most of the field, and, consequently, more chances to birdie. Sadly, just a few tempted him to go for the birdie.

"Most of my shots were 20 to 40 feet away," Woods explained, "because you can't take a run at those flags. You have a wedge in your hands and you're firing 15 feet right or left of the hole. At most Tour events, if you have an 8-iron in your hand, you're going for the flag.

"You have to put the ball in the center of the green here and, hopefully, make a 20- to 30-footer."

Olin Browne (210) got his third par-3 birdie at the 17th.

David Toms (212) birdied the 18th for his 70.

Tiger Woods (213) slumped in frustration at the 16th.

As he saw it, he had only two realistic birdie openings, and he made one, at the 11th. When the putt fell, Woods spread his arms and looked heavenward in gratitude.

Woods had never hidden his emotions, but his putting failures drove him to the brink of desperation. When a putt failed to drop at the 16th, he fell to his knees, his face contorted into a mask of pain, and hung his head.

Nevertheless, even though six strokes and five men separated him from Goosen, only the foolish would dismiss him.

The New Zealander Michael Campbell had played two rounds in 71 and 69, even par for 36 holes, and followed with another 71 in the third, moving him within four strokes of Goosen at the end of the day. He hadn't been this close at this level since he held a two-stroke lead going into the final round of the 1995 British Open. He shot 76 the next day and fell to a tie for third place. John Daly won that championship in a playoff with

Michael Campbell (211) took a share of fourth place after holing out at the 17th for a birdie.

Costantino Rocca. Now Campbell had a chance to win once again.

Campbell opened the third round by holing a nice birdie putt at the first hole, then ran into serious trouble. He missed the second green and saved his par, but he bogeyed three of the next four holes. After missing the third fairway, Campbell needed three more shots to hold the green and bogeyed, missed both fairway and green of the fifth, which was not unusual this day, and caught the green of the sixth and three-putted. A birdie putt fell at the ninth and Campbell escaped with 36, just one over par.

He lost another stroke at the 11th, and looked as if he would drop at least one more when his tee shot to the 17th caught a greenside bunker. Now Campbell played his shot of the round. He dug it out and held his breath as the ball ran right to the heart of the hole for a birdie 2. He closed with a routine par 4 at the home hole, shot his second 71 and at day's end stood amid a strange assortment of men at the front.

Peter Jacobsen (214) had one of the only two 69s.

Third Round

K.J. Choi (213) posted 74 after going three over par on the second nine.

Peter Hedblom (213) birdied the 10th, 11th and 12th.

In the group ahead of Goosen and Browne, Gore had been paired with Choi, who fell back with 74, and with his gallery following, Gore played a struggling 72 spiced by birdies at the fifth and 18th.

Off to an unpromising start, Gore three-putted the first, and when he misdirected his drive into the rough of the fifth, he seemed on his way either to a struggling par or another bogey. But Gore is no weakling. As his fans cheered, he slashed through the heavy grass with a 9-iron, carried his ball 180 yards uphill to within eight feet of the hole and holed the putt. With no more adventures, he played the first nine in 35 strokes. Still, his homeward nine was different.

First, he missed not only the green of the 11th but a four-foot putt that would have saved par. Three holes later he would have settled for no more than a bogey.

No. 2's 14th begins from a high tee and runs straight as a string through menacing rough onto a difficult green. Over four rounds it gave up just 37 birdies, yet claimed 149 bogeys, and 13 holes played in two over par, Gore's among them.

The 13th runs parallel, although in the opposite direction, and Gore had already missed that fairway. From the 14th tee, he looked as if he still wanted to hit it. His ball flew well off to the right, although not as far as the other fairway, and from a lie deep in the grass he had no option but to hack it back into play, still short of the green. His 8-iron left him still without a putt, and he took his 6 and moved on, three over par for the round and losing ground.

He closed out his day on a high note, though, with a big drive that left him 106 yards to the 18th green. A sand-wedge approach set up a putt from 18 feet and he rolled it in.

In some respects, Gore's had been an inconsistent round. He had driven into only five of the 14 fairways and, on the homeward nine, only four greens. Yet he played the second nine in 37, just two over par, saved by his putting. After his loose play at the 14th, he closed out with four consecutive one-putt greens.

Attracted by Gore's attitude as well as his golf, the gallery cheered his every step as he walked those last yards up the 18th fairway. When they saw tears rolling down his cheeks, they cheered even louder, calling, "Go, Jason," or "Go give it to them."

"It's been awesome," Gore said, and when someone asked what he expected on Sunday, he answered, "Well, I expect to be here at 3 o'clock, if that's the last starting time. I hope it's not 2:50."

Goosen had played alongside Olin Browne, who claimed that, in spite of his 72, he had played a horrible round. It had not been inspiring, certainly, but it had its high points. It is unlikely that anyone else in the field birdied three of Pinehurst's four par-3 holes as Browne had that day — the vicious sixth and 15th, and the 17th, milder although not a pushover.

He had played the first nine in 37 and termed his performance atrocious. He claimed as well that his really bad shots left him in playable positions, but his moderately bad shots had settled in "horrible" places.

"It was kind of backwards," he said, "but like I say, I'm hanging on."

Australian Steve Allan (214) was a surprise contender.

Vijay Singh (214) did not have a birdie in his 74.

Arron Oberholser (214) was 'going to have fun.'

Davis Love III (217) had overcome a bad start.

Sergio Garcia (215) fell to a tie for 15th.

His birdie at the sixth, where he holed a 40-foot putt on a very hard par 3, helped make up for his 5 there in the second round, but as his putt crept close to the hole, Browne sensed it drifting away. Instead it caught the lip and toppled in.

He played what he felt was one of his best irons of the day into the ninth, but it carried a yard or two past his target, caught the green's slope and ran off. He bogeyed, dropped another stroke at the 10th, holed from about 12 feet at the 11th to save his par, holed another short putt at the 13th to save a bogey and finished with birdies at the remaining par-3 holes.

Browne shared the last starting time with Goosen, who played as if he faced nothing more than an early match in a club championship rather than a critical round of the game's most demanding competition. Relaxed as ever, he ambled through the course playing mostly first-class shots and the occasional clinker as well. He swept through the first nine with eight 4s and a 3, but played a stretch of loose golf coming in.

Rocco Mediate (215) took a bogey here at the 17th and another at the 18th for his second round of 74.

Losing his grip on his game for a moment, he drove into the rough at the 12th, hit a 7-iron short and left of the green, chipped poorly and lost a stroke, and played the 13th worse. Driving with a 3-wood, he pulled the shot into the left rough, his sand wedge ran over the green and he made 6. From two strokes ahead of Gore after the 11th, Goosen suddenly fell one stroke behind heading for the 14th.

Now Goosen played one of the great shots of this Open. With his drive in a bunker left of the fairway and the ball sitting on an uphill lie, Goosen played a stunning 6-iron shot that flew straight and true onto the green. He holed from 30 feet for a birdie 3 where he might have made any score at all.

From there he played the last four holes in three under par, a surge that climaxed at the 18th. His approach settled short and left of the green, and rather than risk a chancy pitch, Goosen ran the ball onto the green with his putter, hoping for nothing better than a 4, and it dropped into the hole. Back in 34, he shot 69 and, at 207, led the Open by three strokes.

With that kind of margin, he looked unbeatable.

Adam Scott (215) dropped out of the top 10.

Michael Campbell (280) sealed his victory at the 17th by holing a 20-foot putt for a birdie to lead by three strokes.

105th U.S. OPEN
Fourth Round

The final day of the 2005 U.S. Open Championship will be remembered among the wildest fourth rounds within memory. It was a day when Retief Goosen stepped onto the first tee to begin a ceremonial 18 holes before an inevitable coronation that turned into quick abdication, a day when Tiger Woods finally fit together all the parts of his golf swing and stirred the galleries, and principally a day when Michael Campbell redeemed himself for losing the British Open 10 years earlier by winning the U.S. Open with a final round of 69. His total score of 280, even par for Pinehurst No. 2, beat Woods by two strokes and Goosen by eight.

It was also a day when Jason Gore, who had hung around first place for three days, shot 84, and dropped from a tie for second to a tie for 49th place. On Saturday evening, J.L. Lewis was at 224, standing 79th among the 83 players who made the 36-hole cut. At the end of play Lewis had shot 70 and tied Gore.

Olin Browne shot 80 and slipped from a tie with Gore to a tie for 23rd.

At that, Browne out-scored Goosen. After stepping onto the first tee holding a three-stroke lead on scores of 68, 70 and 69, Goosen blundered to an 81, the highest score by a 54-hole Open leader since Gil Morgan's collapse with 81 in 1992. When Goosen finally staggered off the final green, he had sunk to an 11th-place tie.

Anyone who scored around par moved up. Even though he bogeyed two of the last three holes, Woods closed with 69 and finished two strokes behind Campbell with 282. Sergio Garcia shot 70 and, with 285, tied for third with the South African Tim Clark and the Australian Mark Hensby.

Even Davis Love III took a big jump. Left among the debris with his first-round 77, Love played the last three rounds one under par and climbed from a tie for 113th place after the first round into a tie for sixth. No one, by the way, played those last three rounds better, although Campbell and Clark played them in one under par as well.

With Love at 286 were Vijay Singh and Rocco Mediate. Then at 287 came Nick Price and Arron Oberholser, tied for ninth.

Peter Jacobsen had surfaced briefly the previous day but shot 75 and tied for 15th at 289, Ernie Els shot a very good 70 for 289 as well, and Phil Mickelson couldn't recover from his second-round 77, shot 74 and 292 and tied for 33rd. Steve Jones, the 1996 champion, had begun his week with a 69, but he closed with 79 and, with 296, tied for 57th place in a group that included Lee Janzen, the 1993 and 1998 champion. Janzen shot four rounds of 74, which also was the average score of the championship (74.166).

And David Toms went into the last round in position to finish high but slipped to 77 and 289, tied with seven others for 15th.

The gallery assembled early, some fans climbing into the grandstands and claiming seats before the great mass of spectators arrived, bound by the understanding that each person's seat was safe for food breaks and other necessities. An elite few with access had lunch in the old clubhouse, and others with clout went to corporate tents pitched on Maniac Hill, normally Pinehurst's practice range.

Soon word of an ominous weather forecast

Fourth Round

Stewart Cink (289) had one of four 69s.

Fred Couples (289) finished with even-par 70.

Davis Love III (286) overcame a 77 start.

spread through the gallery. A severe electrical storm had been detected moving toward Pinehurst. A USGA staff member headed onto the course in a golf cart loaded with umbrellas, and before long those in the grandstand were told to evacuate and find shelter.

Happily, the storm sidestepped Pinehurst and the Open went ahead as planned.

Among the early starters, only Fred Couples and Stewart Cink picked up any ground at all, and they had gained only one stroke on the early holes. Couples began the day at nine over par and cut it to seven after the 10th, but he lost one stroke at the 14th, another at the 18th and finished the day with an even-par 70 and 289. Cink had played the first three rounds in 10 over, but he found his game and went around in 69. No one played better, and only Love, Campbell and Woods scored as well. Nine men matched par 70, among them Garcia, Clark, Couples, Els and Matt Every.

A 21-year old amateur from Daytona Beach, Fla., Every shot rounds of 75, 73, 73 and 70, and with 291 finished as low amateur, tied for 28th place in a group of five including Adam Scott and Jim Furyk, the 2003 Open champion, and a stroke ahead of Mickelson, Lee Westwood, Bernhard Langer and six others.

Believed to have a decent shot at winning because of his straight driving, Fred Funk looked

Retief Goosen (left, 288) and Jason Gore (294) combined for 165 strokes as they struggled through the afternoon.

overmatched, although he, too, closed with an even-par 70, but his 290 won him only a piece of 23rd place.

And so it went as one after another of the game's leading players fired and fell back.

Not even Woods had a good beginning. He had begun six strokes out of first place, but before he stepped on the third tee, he had fallen eight behind, with bogeys at the first two holes after approach shots only slightly off target. Played too close to the green's treacherous edges, they drifted down slopes and ran yards away from the green. At the first hole he played too cautious a recovery and stared helplessly as the ball rolled back off. On with his fourth shot, he holed a short putt for his 5, and played an encore at the second hole.

Things didn't look good, especially when Campbell, playing two holes behind Woods, opened with a birdie 3, then went into a saving mode. Just as Woods, Campbell missed the second green, but he, instead, salvaged a par.

Sergio Garcia (285) shot 70 and rose to a third-place tie.

Fourth Round

Nick Price (287) was steady — 72, 71, 72, 72.

Tim Clark (285) enjoyed a home advantage.

Fourth Round

Michael Campbell	71 - 69 - 71 - 69 – 280	E
Tiger Woods	70 - 71 - 72 - 69 – 282	+2
Sergio Garcia	71 - 69 - 75 - 70 – 285	+5
Tim Clark	76 - 69 - 70 - 70 – 285	+5
Mark Hensby	71 - 68 - 72 - 74 – 285	+5
Davis Love III	77 - 70 - 70 - 69 – 286	+6
Rocco Mediate	67 - 74 - 74 - 71 – 286	+6
Vijay Singh	70 - 70 - 74 - 72 – 286	+6
Nick Price	72 - 71 - 72 - 72 – 287	+7
Arron Oberholser	76 - 67 - 71 - 73 – 287	+7
Bob Estes	70 - 73 - 75 - 70 – 288	+8
Corey Pavin	73 - 72 - 70 - 73 – 288	+8
Peter Hedblom	77 - 66 - 70 - 75 – 288	+8
Retief Goosen	68 - 70 - 69 - 81 – 288	+8

At the time, all this seemed a sideshow, with Goosen so far ahead and playing a superb brand of golf. Smooth as ever, he ripped his first drive down the fairway, and from about 120 yards out held the green with his approach, played a nice first putt inside a foot and made his 4, ho-hum.

Suddenly the mood changed. Once again Goosen's drive settled in the fairway of the second, but after changing clubs, his approach caught the wrong part of the green. Like Woods at the first, his approach rolled off the right side of the green, leaving him a delicate shot to the hole.

By then it had become clear that No. 2 demanded links golf, that is, rolling the ball onto the green instead of playing lofted shots. Links golf is, after all, a ground game.

Unfortunately, Goosen rolled his ball too far. It scooted off the far side like a runaway train, and for a heart-stopping moment his second attempt looked as if it might as well. Instead, it pulled up short of danger, and Goosen got down in two putts. He had dropped two strokes on one hole, and then lost another at the third, where once again his ball slipped off the green, he played a timid first putt and missed with the second. Three strokes gone in two holes, and now Goosen had turned a runaway into a tight, tense battle.

Up ahead, Singh had run off three consecutive

Mark Hensby (285) kept his top-five place.

Vijay Singh (286) hit only five fairways.

birdies and closed within two strokes of Goosen. Campbell had caught Goosen at even par, and even though he had lost a stroke, Hensby moved into third place at two over par, tied with Singh and Browne. Gore held on at three over, and Woods and Toms followed at four over par. Pinehurst was taking its toll.

It struck Singh at the eighth, where his long first putt gathered speed as it passed the hole and ran off the back. He took three more to hole out and, with a 6, dropped from sight. Toms had lost three strokes on the first two holes and gone out in 40, Browne and Gore played gamely but had nothing left, and Goosen had collapsed. The Open would be left to Campbell and Woods, although two unlikely challengers refused to give up.

Hensby had played through three rounds in 211, tied with Campbell, but Tim Clark began the last round eight strokes behind Goosen, at 215, apparently hopelessly out of the chase. A short, 5-foot-7 South African, whose long putter reaches to his chin, Clark attended North Carolina State University, whose campus in Raleigh isn't far from

Matt Every (291) shot 70 to be the low amateur.

Arron Oberholser (287) posted 34 on the last nine.

Ryuji Imada (289) rose after starting with 77.

Corey Pavin (288) was rewarded for his long trip.

Peter Hedblom (288) had an up-and-down week.

Pinehurst. A resident of Scottsdale, Ariz., who played mainly on the Nationwide Tour, Clark climbed close to the leaders simply by playing par golf through the first nine.

Hensby probably is best known for having parked his car in Chicago's Cog Hill Golf Club parking lot for a few weeks and used it as his bedroom. That, of course, is behind him. Safely on the PGA Tour, he tied for fifth place in the Masters early in the year, but had done nothing of note since. Now here he was in position to win the Open.

In the end, though, neither Clark nor Hensby made any difference. Nor did Goosen, Gore or Browne. The championship evolved into a battle of wills between Woods, who had won it twice, and Campbell, who had missed the cut in his last four attempts.

As the last round unfolded, Campbell had played better shots into the greens than either Goosen or Woods. Their approaches landed hard and occasionally ran away. Campbell's hit softly and held. It seems reasonable to state as well that his

Tiger Woods (282) holed a short putt for a birdie at the seventh to be three strokes off the lead.

overall shot-making and putting surpassed theirs.

Take No. 2's fifth hole, a rugged par 4 of 472 yards with a green sitting well above the landing area. Beginning his round ahead of Campbell, Woods played two superb shots into the green. From 185 yards out, his approach ran over the green, he putted back on and holed from 12 feet for his par.

Moments later, Campbell pulled his drive into the left rough, and with no chance of hitting the green, pitched close to the front, played a crisp pitch that hit the green and bit close to the hole, and holed for his par as well.

Even par then, Campbell led Woods by four strokes, but now Woods played a monstrous drive to the seventh that cleared a stand of towering pines at the turn of the left-to-right dogleg that left nothing but a short pitch on a hole of just over 400 yards. He birdied. Three behind now.

Then Woods stumbled at the ninth, left his tee shot short and bogeyed. He had gone out in 36, a stroke above par, and once again fell four strokes behind.

Campbell, here at the fourth, was saving pars.

Fourth Round

Woods took three putts for a bogey at the 17th.

Then Campbell could bogey and win by two strokes.

Campbell, meanwhile, pulled his drive into the gallery at the eighth, but suddenly the ball came shooting out and into the rough. Word spread that the ball had caromed off a woman's head on the first bounce. Perhaps. Whatever, Campbell bogeyed, saved his par at the ninth with a deft chip close to the hole and made the turn in 35, a stroke better than Woods, but now Woods trailed by three.

Now, as the Open went into its final nine holes, the tension climbed, and Woods made his move.

His big drive split the fairway of the 10th, the 607-yard par 5, and left him 265 yards from the green. Astounding the galleries, Woods rocketed a 4-iron into the right greenside bunker, his recovery just skimmed past the hole, and he birdied. Two strokes behind.

Another long drive left him just 125 yards to the 11th green, a tough par 4 of 476 yards. His pitch hit past the hole with so much backspin it drew back within three feet of the hole. Another birdie. One stroke behind.

The gallery raced ahead to the 12th, its cheers heard throughout the course telling everyone that Woods was on the march. No one knew yet, though, that his charge had stalled at the 12th. He played through the 14th with nothing but pars.

While Woods picked up strokes, Campbell played solid golf as well. His second shot to the long 10th settled right of the green, he pitched to 25 feet, then holed for a birdie of his own. Putting beautifully, he conceded nothing. His approach to the 11th caught the left side of the green and drifted into a bunker, he pitched out to about five feet and holed yet another dicey putt for the 4.

With another big drive within 100 yards of the 12th green, Campbell pitched within birdie range and holed once again. One under par now, but with six hard holes ahead.

Another routine par at the 13th and another at the 14th. Campbell had played the first 14 holes in one under, but No. 2's most harrowing holes lay ahead.

As the crowd at the 18th erupted in cheers, Campbell looked to the heavens in an emotional finish.

The green of the 15th, a 203-yard par 3, had been perhaps the most difficult of all to hold, and the 16th, which measured 492 yards, was Pinehurst's longest. Normally it plays as a par 5 of over 500 yards, but since golfers of Open caliber can reach the green with hardly more than a 5-iron — Woods, for example, played a 9-iron — the USGA moved to a forward tee and properly designated par as 4.

Now Woods began that final run for home with a gorgeous 6-iron into the 15th that hit softly left of the hole and set up a birdie opening. He holed for a 2. Down to one over par, he trailed Campbell by two strokes, moving in. At a time when it looked that Woods might win, he instead let it slip away.

Woods drove into the right rough of the 16th in grass so dense he couldn't reach the green with his second, played a loose chip and two-putted for a bogey 5.

One hole later, at the short 17th, his tee shot settled within 20 feet and he three-putted. His birdie 3 at the home hole meant little unless Campbell stumbled.

He didn't. Campbell bogeyed the 16th, but he sealed the victory with a 20-foot putt at the 17th that ran straight and true right into the center of the hole.

Three strokes ahead now, Campbell could afford to lay up safely from a tough lie in the 18th hole's left rough, and even though he putted twice from nowhere at the home green for a final bogey 5, he had won the championship by two strokes.

Campbell deserved to win simply because he played better than anyone. He hit quality shots. He drove well, he played first-class irons, he putted like a dream, and he refused to wilt under the pressure of Woods's challenge. In the end it was Woods who buckled.

His championship secure, Campbell pulled his cap down and across his face to hide the welling tears as he strode off the final green, at ease now that four hard days over a tough golf course had ended in glory.

Michael Campbell cradled the U.S. Open trophy and was thrilled that his name would go alongside those inscribed.

Ten years before he won the U.S. Open Championship, Michael Campbell introduced himself by shooting 65 over the St. Andrews Old Course and leading the third round of the 1995 British Open. That he had played this well at St. Andrews added to his celebrity. After 71s in the opening two rounds, Campbell rose to first place with a third round that featured seven 3s, six of them over a seven-hole run from the seventh through the 14th. He played all the rest in 4s.

In one unforgettable moment he put his round at risk by attempting an improbable shot from the Road Bunker, a sand pit left of the 17th green that has brought grief to many a player more notable than Campbell. The bunker's face rises sharply straight upward, held together by stacked layers of sod. To those standing near the first green, the bunker's face appeared higher than Campbell's head. As he watched what he saw as an act of sheer folly, Tim Treacy fumed. An official of the New Zealand Golf Association, Treacy growled, "If he leaves that ball in the bunker I'll wring his neck."

Campbell's recovery did indeed clear that sheer wall and he saved his par 4. The next day he shot 76 and dropped into a tie for third, behind John Daly, the new champion, and Costantino Rocca, the loser in a four-hole playoff.

Campbell had been 26 years old, and within a year had slipped from view. Since then not much had been heard from him in the United States until that riveting final round at Pinehurst when he played such nerveless golf, stared down Tiger Woods, left Retief Goosen in the dust and won the 2005 U.S. Open.

Campbell became the second New Zealander to win one of the game's jewels. Bob Charles had been the first, 42 years earlier in the 1963 British Open, not only the first New Zealander but the first left-hander to win one of golf's greatest prizes. Campbell also became the latest of the U.S. Open's 23 foreign-born champions, responsible for a total of 29 championships.

After hoisting the U.S. Open trophy overhead, Campbell marveled, "I think for the first time I actually made the front page of the newspapers back home with the All Blacks," New Zealand's great national rugby team, named for their all-black uniforms. "They've been champions and heroes of mine, and to knock them off the front pages for this one week means a lot to me."

In an emotional moment as he left the final green, hat pulled over his face and tears running down his cheeks, Michael thought, "It's been a journey, my career." Explaining later, he said, "I was thinking about people back home in New Zealand, and my wife, who is in England right now, Julie, and my two boys, Thomas and Jordan, because they couldn't be with me. And obviously Father's Day, my dad watching me back home, and the family."

With a nut-brown complexion and black hair, Campbell is a Maori, a Polynesian people indigenous to New Zealand. "I'm very proud to be who I am," Campbell told reporters. "Winning a major championship for the Kiwis is going to be a great thing for the game of golf back home, especially for the Maori people."

Steve Williams, Tiger Woods's caddie, is also a New Zealander, from Wellington, Campbell's home town. Waiting behind the final green as

The Champion

Campbell finished, Williams put his arms around him and said, "You've made a lot of people back home very, very proud."

Then, turning to reporters, Williams said, "This was a huge day for the Maori. They've never had anything like this to celebrate. Never anything like it!" In what seemed an exaggeration, he compared Campbell's winning the Open to Sir Edmund Hillary's 1953 climb to the peak of Mount Everest. Hillary, of course, was a New Zealander as well.

Back in New Zealand, the commentary ran wild.

"The jokes can stop now," one gushed. "Even the tag about (Campbell as) the best Maori golfer never to win a major (championship)." Describing those Campbell had beaten, the writer suggested, "Those were the players who could only stand and watch as a proud Maori New Zealander did something very special."

Woods himself predicted, "Michael is going to have a wonderful welcome when he goes home, as well he should." In a way, Campbell had taken one giant step to trump two runner-up losses to Woods. He had lost to him by four strokes in both the 2001 Deutsche Bank-SAP Open in Germany and the 2002 Bay Hill Invitational.

Whether or not Campbell thought of those tournaments or of Hillary wasn't made clear, but he did indeed think of Charles as he finished. "To be in the same circle, the same sentence, as Bob Charles is an honor for me," he said.

Emphasizing his roots on the Open's final day, Campbell wore a white shirt designed for him by the Maori-owned Kai Kaha Clothing Company, which carries a "Cambo" line. In the Maori language, the company name means inner strength, and the motif of the shirt was described as a contemporary Maori design incorporating the mango pare, or hammerhead shark.

Campbell's name, however, came straight out of Scotland. In the mid-19th century, Sir Logan Campbell left Edinburgh and sailed to New Zealand. Over the years he married several wives, at least one a Maori, which explains how Michael became a Campbell. Sir Logan is Michael's great-great-great-grandfather.

"That's where the name Cambo comes from," he said. "It's Scottish. It's in my blood to play golf."

Drawn to the game as a young man, Michael developed into an outstanding amateur golfer, won the Australian and New South Wales Amateur Championships and represented New Zealand in the 1992 World Amateur Team Championship, played that year in Vancouver, B.C. Not only did New Zealand win by seven strokes over the United States, but Campbell shot 272 over the four rounds and turned in the second lowest individual score, one stroke behind his teammate, Phil Tataurangi.

Campbell's shirt featured a Maori design.

Campbell built on that beginning and the following year played so well on the Australasian Tour as a professional he was named its rookie of the year.

Strangely enough, Campbell had thought of quitting seven years before he won the Open. By 1998 he couldn't score, often shot in the 80s, lost his entrée to the European Tour and thought of quitting.

"I just could not play the game," he said. "I could not focus on what I was doing. I could not swing the golf club."

His frustration simmering, one night he threw

his golf bag across a hotel room and told himself, "It's all over." Discouraged, he had given up and, he said, "I was about to chop them in pieces and throw them away."

Campbell had lost his game partly because he had injured his left wrist. Toward the end of 1995 he played eight tournaments in seven countries without a break.

"Maybe it was greed, maybe I wanted to expose myself too much," he admitted. Then, playing in the New Zealand Open in December, springtime in the southern hemisphere, something snapped in his left wrist. Apparently a tendon broke away from the bone, and for months, he said, he couldn't hold a club, couldn't even hold a knife and fork.

The injury healed over time, and soon he began playing well again, partly because he had been driven to practice by Jonathan Yarwood, his coach, and Michael Waite, his caddie. He began playing so much better he revived his career and regained his status as a regular member of the European and Australasian tours.

It was also during this time, in 1996, that Campbell married. He and Julie had two sons (Thomas in 1998 and Jordan in 2000).

With his U.S. Open credentials, he considered re-joining the PGA Tour. He had played two years ago, dragging his wife and kids through the country with no real roots. Evidently a devoted family man, he'd had enough and took his family back to England.

Between his near-miss at St. Andrews and the 2005 U.S. Open, Campbell had won eight tournaments on the European and Australasian tours, his first in the Johnnie Walker Classic in Taiwan, where his revival began in November 1999 with that European-sanctioned event.

Campbell shot 66-71-69-70–276 and won over a field that included Ernie Els, who had won two U.S. Opens by then, Vijay Singh, the current PGA champion, and Woods, trying to win his fifth successive tournament.

The following year he won the German Masters on the European Tour and three more in Australasia, among them the New Zealand Open, making him especially proud. Tied at 269 with Craig Perks, another New Zealander, Campbell holed an 18-foot eagle putt on the second playoff hole at Paraparaumu Beach, a linksland course about 35 miles north of Wellington.

Including the New Zealand Open, Campbell won three tournaments in four weeks — the Heineken Classic in Perth, on Australia's west coast, and the Ericsson Masters, in Melbourne, in southeastern Australia's sand belt.

Success bred success, and Campbell later won the 2001 Heineken Classic, the 2002 European Open and the 2003 Irish Open. By then he had developed into a consistent money winner, at first well down the European Tour's Order of Merit — money winnings — but climbing. He rose from 133rd in 1997, to fourth in 2000, his peak, and finished 2004 in 28th place.

Coming into 2005, Campbell had won over £4.5 million in Europe, including £1 million in 2000 alone, and never under £500,000 since. Add what he had won in Australasia and he had won over $1 million every year for six years, a string that includes 2005 as well.

After his banner 2000 season, Campbell was named to the Queen's Birthday Honours List. Since both Hillary and Charles have been knighted, perhaps Campbell will eventually follow them and come full circle to Sir Logan.

At 5-foot-9 and 190 pounds, Campbell is built for golf. He has a fluid, compact swing, drove the ball long enough at Pinehurst — he averaged just over 294 yards on the two measured holes — played skillful irons and putted out of his mind over the last nine holes, with six one-putt greens.

He maintains homes in Wellington, at the southern end of New Zealand's north island, and in Brighton, England, where Julie remained with their sons while Michael made history. She called him the Sunday morning of the final round.

"Are you ready for this one?" she asked.

"Yeah, yeah," he said, "I am ready."

Unconvinced, she insisted, "No, Michael. Are you *really* ready for this one?"

"Yeah," he answered, "I am *really* ready for this one."

And so he was.

105th U.S. OPEN Pinehurst

June 16-19, 2005, Pinehurst No. 2, Pinehurst, N.C.

Rd. 1	Rd. 2	Rd. 3	Rd. 4	Contestant	Rounds				Total	Prize
T17	T6	T4	1	Michael Campbell	71	69	71	69	280	$1,170,000.00
T10	T10	T7	2	Tiger Woods	70	71	72	69	282	700,000.00
T17	T6	T15	T3	Sergio Garcia	71	69	75	70	285	320,039.00
T94	T33	T15	T3	Tim Clark	76	69	70	70	285	320,039.00
T17	T4	T4	T3	Mark Hensby	71	68	72	74	285	320,039.00
T113	T57	T26	T6	Davis Love III	77	70	70	69	286	187,813.00
T1	T10	T15	T6	Rocco Mediate	67	74	74	71	286	187,813.00
T10	T6	T11	T6	Vijay Singh	70	70	74	72	286	187,813.00
T32	T20	T15	T9	Nick Price	72	71	72	72	287	150,834.00
T94	T20	T11	T9	Arron Oberholser	76	67	71	73	287	150,834.00
T10	T20	R35	T11	Bob Estes	70	73	75	70	288	123,857.00
T46	T33	T15	T11	Corey Pavin	73	72	70	73	288	123,857.00
T113	T20	T7	T11	Peter Hedblom	77	66	70	75	288	123,857.00
T3	T1	1	T11	Retief Goosen	68	70	69	81	288	123,857.00
T46	T57	T48	T15	Stewart Cink	73	74	73	69	289	88,120.00
T17	T33	T41	T15	Fred Couples	71	74	74	70	289	88,120.00
T17	T57	T41	T15	Ernie Els	71	76	72	70	289	88,120.00
T113	T33	T35	T15	Ryuji Imada	77	68	73	71	289	88,120.00
T17	T57	T26	T15	John Cook	71	76	70	72	289	88,120.00
T32	T33	T11	T15	Peter Jacobsen	72	73	69	75	289	88,120.00
T6	T4	T7	T15	K.J. Choi	69	70	74	76	289	88,120.00
T10	T17	6	T15	David Toms	70	72	70	77	289	88,120.00
T46	T28	T48	T23	Fred Funk	73	71	76	70	290	59,633.00
T94	T57	T26	T23	Justin Leonard	76	71	70	73	290	59,633.00
T32	T28	T21	T23	Paul Claxton	72	72	72	74	290	59,633.00
T75	T33	T21	T23	Kenny Perry	75	70	71	74	290	59,633.00
T1	T1	T2	T23	Olin Browne	67	71	72	80	290	59,633.00
T75	T72	T57	T28	*Matt Every	75	73	73	70	291	Medal
T32	T45	T26	T28	Geoff Ogilvy	72	74	71	74	291	44,486.00
T17	T10	T21	T28	Jim Furyk	71	70	75	75	291	44,486.00
T10	T10	T15	T28	Adam Scott	70	71	74	76	291	44,486.00
T32	T10	T11	T28	Steve Allan	72	69	73	77	291	44,486.00
T54	T20	T63	T33	Steve Elkington	74	69	79	70	292	35,759.00
T3	T10	T48	T33	Brandt Jobe	68	73	79	72	292	35,759.00
T6	T45	T35	T33	Phil Mickelson	69	77	72	74	292	35,759.00
T54	T57	T35	T33	Bernhard Langer	74	73	71	74	292	35,759.00
T17	T28	T26	T33	Angel Cabrera	71	73	73	75	292	35,759.00
T46	T28	T26	T33	Ted Purdy	73	71	73	75	292	35,759.00
T17	T33	T26	T33	Shigeki Maruyama	71	74	72	75	292	35,759.00
T54	T57	T26	T33	Tim Herron	74	73	70	75	292	35,759.00
T3	T6	T7	T33	Lee Westwood	68	72	73	79	292	35,759.00
T75	T57	T63	T42	Mike Weir	75	72	75	71	293	26,223.00
T54	T57	T48	T42	Tom Pernice	74	73	73	73	293	26,223.00
T113	T72	T48	T42	Chad Campbell	77	71	72	73	293	26,223.00
T17	T33	T41	T42	Peter Lonard	71	74	74	74	293	26,223.00
T54	T45	T41	T42	Rob Rashell	74	72	73	74	293	26,223.00
T32	T57	T41	T42	Colin Montgomerie	72	75	72	74	293	26,223.00
T94	T72	T41	T42	Paul McGinley	76	72	71	74	293	26,223.00

105th U.S. Open

Rd. 1	Rd. 2	Rd. 3	Rd. 4	Contestant	Rounds				Total	Prize
T75	T72	79	T49	J.L. Lewis	75	73	76	70	294	20,275.00
T32	T20	T57	T49	Nick O'Hern	72	71	78	73	294	20,275.00
T17	T1	T2	T49	Jason Gore	71	67	72	84	294	20,275.00
T32	T28	T63	T52	Richard Green	72	72	78	73	295	17,667.00
T54	T33	T63	T52	Soren Kjeldsen	74	71	77	73	295	17,667.00
T75	T72	T57	T52	Thomas Levet	75	73	73	74	295	17,667.00
T17	T33	T48	T52	Thomas Bjorn	71	74	75	75	295	17,667.00
T32	T45	T48	T52	Nick Dougherty	72	74	74	75	295	17,667.00
T75	T72	T82	T57	Frank Lickliter II	75	73	78	70	296	15,223.00
T75	T72	T75	T57	*Ryan Moore	75	73	75	73	296	
T46	T45	T63	T57	J.J. Henry	73	73	76	74	296	15,223.00
T54	T72	T63	T57	Lee Janzen	74	74	74	74	296	15,223.00
T10	T17	T57	T57	Tommy Armour III	70	72	79	75	296	15,223.00
T32	T45	T57	T57	Jonathan Lomas	72	74	75	75	296	15,223.00
T113	T45	T48	T57	Ian Poulter	77	69	74	76	296	15,223.00
T6	T20	T26	T57	Steve Jones	69	74	74	79	296	15,223.00
T54	T10	T21	T57	Keiichiro Fukabori	74	67	75	80	296	15,223.00
T6	T17	T21	T57	Luke Donald	69	73	74	80	296	15,223.00
T46	T33	T63	T67	Michael Allen	73	72	77	75	297	13,553.00
T32	T20	T57	T67	Steve Flesch	72	71	78	76	297	13,553.00
T54	T45	T41	T67	John Mallinger	74	72	73	78	297	13,553.00
T54	T57	T35	T67	Bill Glasson	74	73	71	79	297	13,553.00
T17	T45	T63	T71	Stephen Ames	71	75	76	76	298	12,551.00
T32	T45	T63	T71	Rory Sabbatini	72	74	76	76	298	12,551.00
T54	T57	T63	T71	D.J. Brigman	74	73	75	76	298	12,551.00
T113	T72	T63	T71	J.P. Hayes	77	71	74	76	298	12,551.00
T54	T45	T75	T75	John Daly	74	72	77	76	299	11,674.00
T75	T72	T75	T75	Omar Uresti	75	73	75	76	299	11,674.00
T113	T33	T35	T75	Charles Howell	77	68	73	81	299	11,674.00
T17	T45	T80	T78	Bob Tway	71	75	79	75	300	11,048.00
T32	T57	T63	T78	Jeff Maggert	72	75	75	78	300	11,048.00
T94	T72	T82	T80	Chris Nallen	76	72	78	75	301	10,547.00
T54	T72	T48	T80	Graeme McDowell	74	74	72	81	301	10,547.00
T94	T57	T75	82	Craig Barlow	76	71	76	80	303	10,171.00
T94	T57	T80	83	Jerry Kelly	76	71	78	80	305	9,921.00

Contestant	R1	R2	Tot	Contestant	R1	R2	Tot	Contestant	R1	R2	Tot
Peter Hanson	76	73	149	Ian Leggatt	75	76	151	Joe Ogilvie	79	75	154
Shingo Katayama	74	75	149	Eric Axley	81	70	151	Rich Beem	78	76	154
Robert Allenby	72	77	149	Nick Gilliam	76	75	151	Brandt Snedeker	79	75	154
Carlos Franco	74	75	149	David Oh	74	77	151	Scott McCarron	76	78	154
Tom Lehman	77	72	149	James Driscoll	76	75	151	*David Denham	77	77	154
Robert Karlsson	75	74	149	Shaun Micheel	78	74	152	Robert Gamez	77	78	155
Zach Johnson	74	75	149	Stuart Appleby	81	71	152	Scott Gibson	77	78	155
Toru Taniguchi	70	79	149	David Duval	76	76	152	Nick Jones	80	75	155
Euan Walters	76	73	149	Craig Parry	77	75	152	Len Mattiace	76	79	155
Jerry Smith	78	71	149	Jay Haas	82	70	152	*Michael Putnam	76	79	155
Derek Brown	75	74	149	Steve Lowery	78	74	152	Franklin Langham	74	81	155
John Rollins	75	74	149	Steven Conran	77	75	152	Ben Curtis	76	80	156
Matt Kuchar	75	74	149	Patrick Damron	79	73	152	Aaron Barber	74	82	156
Todd Hamilton	75	74	149	Kyle Willmann	75	77	152	David Hearn	77	79	156
Eric Meichtry	75	74	149	Miguel A. Jimenez	79	74	153	Simon Dyson	79	78	157
Spencer Levin	73	77	150	Carl Pettersson	77	76	153	Michael Ruiz	79	79	158
*Trip Kuehne	75	75	150	Bart Bryant	79	74	153	*Lee Williams	79	79	158
Jose-Filipe Lima	75	75	150	Casey Wittenberg	75	78	153	Jim Benepe	82	76	158
John Merrick	77	73	150	Clint Jensen	77	76	153	Rod Pampling	80	79	159
Scott Verplank	76	74	150	Yong Eun Yang	74	79	153	*Pierre-Henri Soero	83	77	160
Lee Rinker	76	74	150	*Luke List	82	71	153	Sal Spallone	79	81	160
Troy Kelly	83	67	150	Chris DiMarco	71	82	153	Wil Collins	82	79	161
Padraig Harrington	77	74	151	Scott Parel	76	77	153	Conrad Ray	80	84	164
Stephen Gallacher	79	72	151	Josh McCumber	73	80	153	David Howell	74		WD
								Paul Casey	85		WD

Professionals not returning 72-hole scores received $2,000 each.   *Denotes amateur.

105th U.S. OPEN Statistics

Hole	1	2	3	4	5	6	7	8	9	10	11	12	13	14	15	16	17	18	Total	
Par	4	4	4	5	4	3	4	4	3	5	4	4	4	4	3	4	3	4	70	
Michael Campbell																				
Round 1	4	[5]	4	(4)	4	[4]	[5]	(3)	3	5	4	4	(3)	[5]	3	4	3	4	71	
Round 2	4	4	(3)	(4)	[5]	3	(3)	4	[4]	(4)	[5]	[5]	(3)	[5]	3	4	(2)	4	69	
Round 3	(3)	4	[5]	5	[5]	[4]	4	4	(2)	5	[5]	4	4	4	3	4	(2)	4	71	
Round 4	(3)	4	4	5	4	3	4	[5]	3	(4)	4	(3)	4	4	3	[5]	(2)	[5]	69	280
Tiger Woods																				
Round 1	4	4	4	(4)	4	3	4	4	3	(4)	4	4	4	4	[4]	[5]	3	4	70	
Round 2	4	(3)	[5]	(4)	4	[4]	4	[5]	[4]	5	4	4	4	4	3	(3)	3	4	71	
Round 3	[5]	4	[5]	5	4	3	4	4	3	5	(3)	[5]	4	4	3	4	3	4	72	
Round 4	[5]	[5]	4	(4)	4	3	(3)	4	[4]	(4)	(3)	4	4	4	(2)	[5]	[4]	(3)	69	282
Retief Goosen																				
Round 1	4	4	4	(4)	4	3	4	4	3	(4)	4	4	(3)	[5]	3	4	3	4	68	
Round 2	(3)	4	4	(4)	[5]	3	[5]	4	3	(4)	4	4	4	4	[4]	4	3	4	70	
Round 3	4	4	4	(4)	4	[4]	4	4	3	5	(3)	[5]	[6]	(3)	(2)	4	3	(3)	69	
Round 4	4	[6]	[5]	5	[5]	[4]	4	4	[4]	5	4	[5]	[5]	[5]	[4]	[5]	3	4	81	288

○ Circled numbers represent birdies or eagles.   □ Squared numbers represent bogeys or worse.

Hole	Yards	Par	Eagles	Birdies	Pars	Bogeys	Double Bogeys	Higher	Average
1	401	4	0	46	308	116	6	0	4.172
2	469	4	0	26	244	173	28	5	4.458
3	336	4	1	72	313	76	12	2	4.069
4	565	5	5	155	270	44	1	1	4.756
5	472	4	0	28	253	175	19	1	4.395
6	220	3	0	22	288	159	5	2	3.321
7	404	4	0	46	309	110	10	1	4.183
8	467	4	0	24	293	144	14	1	4.317
9	175	3	1	51	299	105	16	4	3.202
OUT	3,509	35	7	470	2,577	1,102	111	17	36.873
10	607	5	3	88	282	88	14	1	5.053
11	476	4	0	23	290	150	12	1	4.324
12	449	4	0	42	286	131	13	4	4.267
13	378	4	0	74	278	106	18	0	4.143
14	468	4	0	37	274	149	13	3	4.311
15	203	3	0	25	264	178	8	1	3.361
16	492	4	0	22	256	173	23	2	4.426
17	190	3	0	40	335	96	4	1	3.141
18	442	4	0	36	298	123	17	2	4.267
IN	3,705	35	3	387	2,563	1,194	122	15	37.293
TOTAL	7,214	70	10	857	5,140	2,296	233	32	74.166

105th U.S. OPEN
Past Results

Date	Winner	Score	Runner-Up	Venue
1895	Horace Rawlins	173 - 36 holes	Willie Dunn	Newport GC, Newport, R.I.
1896	James Foulis	152 - 36 holes	Horace Rawlins	Shinnecock Hills GC, Southampton, N.Y.
1897	Joe Lloyd	162 - 36 holes	Willie Anderson	Chicago GC, Wheaton, Ill.
1898	Fred Herd	328 - 72 holes	Alex Smith	Myopia Hunt Club, S. Hamilton, Mass.
1899	Willie Smith	315	George Low Val Fitzjohn W.H. Way	Baltimore CC, Baltimore, Md.
1900	Harry Vardon	313	J.H. Taylor	Chicago GC, Wheaton, Ill.
1901	*Willie Anderson (85)	331	Alex Smith (86)	Myopia Hunt Club, S. Hamilton, Mass.
1902	Laurie Auchterlonie	307	Stewart Gardner	Garden City GC, Garden City, N.Y.
1903	*Willie Anderson (82)	307	David Brown (84)	Baltusrol GC, Springfield, N.J.
1904	Willie Anderson	303	Gil Nicholls	Glen View Club, Golf, Ill.
1905	Willie Anderson	314	Alex Smith	Myopia Hunt Club, S. Hamilton, Mass.
1906	Alex Smith	295	Willie Smith	Onwentsia Club, Lake Forest, Ill.
1907	Alex Ross	302	Gil Nicholls	Philadelphia Cricket Club, Chestnut Hill, Pa.
1908	*Fred McLeod (77)	322	Willie Smith (83)	Myopia Hunt Club, S. Hamilton, Mass.
1909	George Sargent	290	Tom McNamara	Englewood GC, Englewood, N.J.
1910	*Alex Smith (71)	298	John J. McDermott (75) Macdonald Smith (77)	Philadelphia Cricket Club, Chestnut Hill, Pa.
1911	*John J. McDermott (80)	307	Michael J. Brady (82) George O. Simpson (85)	Chicago GC, Wheaton, Ill.
1912	John J. McDermott	294	Tom McNamara	CC of Buffalo, Buffalo, N.Y.
1913	*Francis Ouimet (72)	304	Harry Vardon (77) Edward Ray (78)	The Country Club, Brookline, Mass.
1914	Walter Hagen	290	Charles Evans Jr.	Midlothian CC, Blue Island, Ill.
1915	Jerome D. Travers	297	Tom McNamara	Baltusrol GC, Springfield, N.J.
1916	Charles Evans Jr.	286	Jock Hutchinson	Minikahda Club, Minneapolis, Minn.
1917-18	No Championships Played — World War I			
1919	*Walter Hagen (77)	301	Michael J. Brady (78)	Brae Burn CC, West Newton, Mass.
1920	Edward Ray	295	Harry Vardon Jack Burke, Sr. Leo Diegel Jock Hutchison	Inverness Club, Toledo, Ohio
1921	James M. Barnes	289	Walter Hagen Fred McLeod	Columbia CC, Chevy Chase, Md.
1922	Gene Sarazen	288	John L. Black Robert T. Jones Jr.	Skokie CC, Glencoe, Ill.
1923	*Robert T. Jones Jr. (76)	296	Bobby Cruickshank (78)	Inwood CC, Inwood, N.Y.
1924	Cyril Walker	297	Robert T. Jones Jr.	Oakland Hills CC, Birmingham, Mich.
1925	*William Macfarlane (147)	291	Robert T. Jones Jr. (148)	Worcester CC, Worcester, Mass.
1926	Robert T. Jones Jr.	293	Joe Turnesa	Scioto CC, Columbus, Ohio
1927	*Tommy Armour (76)	301	Harry Cooper (79)	Oakmont CC, Oakmont, Pa.
1928	*Johnny Farrell (143)	294	Robert T. Jones Jr. (144)	Olympia Fields CC, Matteson, Ill.
1929	*Robert T. Jones Jr. (141)	294	Al Espinosa (164)	Winged Foot GC, Mamaroneck, N.Y.

Past Results

Date	Winner	Score	Runner-Up	Venue
1930	Robert T. Jones Jr.	287	Macdonald Smith	Interlachen CC, Hopkins, Minn.
1931	*Billy Burke (149-148)	292	George Von Elm (149-149)	Inverness Club, Toledo, Ohio
1932	Gene Sarazen	286	Phil Perkins Bobby Cruickshank	Fresh Meadows CC, Flushing, N.Y.
1933	Johnny Goodman	287	Ralph Guldahl	North Shore CC, Glenview, Ill.
1934	Olin Dutra	293	Gene Sarazen	Merion Cricket Club, Ardmore, Pa.
1935	Sam Parks Jr.	299	Jimmy Thomson	Oakmont CC, Oakmont, Pa.
1936	Tony Manero	282	Harry Cooper	Baltusrol GC, Springfield, N.J.
1937	Ralph Guldahl	281	Sam Snead	Oakland Hills CC, Birmingham, Mich.
1938	Ralph Guldahl	284	Dick Metz	Cherry Hills CC, Englewood, Col.
1939	*Byron Nelson (68-70)	284	Craig Wood (68-73) Denny Shute (76)	Philadelphia CC, West Conshohocken, Pa.
1940	*Lawson Little (70)	287	Gene Sarazen (73)	Canterbury GC, Cleveland, Ohio
1941	Craig Wood	284	Denny Shute	Colonial Club, Fort Worth, Texas
1942-45	No Championships Played — World War II			
1946	*Lloyd Mangrum (72-72)	284	Vic Ghezzi (72-73) Byron Nelson (72-73)	Canterbury GC, Cleveland, Ohio
1947	*Lew Worsham (69)	282	Sam Snead (70)	St. Louis CC, Clayton, Mo.
1948	Ben Hogan	276	Jimmy Demaret	Riviera CC, Los Angeles, Calif.
1949	Cary Middlecoff	286	Sam Snead Clayton Heafner	Medinah CC, Medinah, Ill.
1950	*Ben Hogan (69)	287	Lloyd Mangrum (73) George Fazio (75)	Merion GC, Ardmore, Pa.
1951	Ben Hogan	287	Clayton Heafner	Oakland Hills CC, Birmingham, Mich.
1952	Julius Boros	281	Ed (Porky) Oliver	Northwood CC, Dallas, Texas
1953	Ben Hogan	283	Sam Snead	Oakmont CC, Oakmont, Pa.
1954	Ed Furgol	284	Gene Littler	Baltusrol GC, Springfield, N.J.
1955	*Jack Fleck (69)	287	Ben Hogan (72)	The Olympic Club, San Francisco, Calif.
1956	Cary Middlecoff	281	Ben Hogan Julius Boros	Oak Hill CC, Rochester, N.Y.
1957	*Dick Mayer (72)	282	Cary Middlecoff (79)	Inverness Club, Toledo, Ohio
1958	Tommy Bolt	283	Gary Player	Southern Hills CC, Tulsa, Okla.
1959	Billy Casper	282	Bob Rosburg	Winged Foot GC, Mamaroneck, N.Y.
1960	Arnold Palmer	280	Jack Nicklaus	Cherry Hills CC, Englewood, Col.
1961	Gene Littler	281	Bob Goalby Doug Sanders	Oakland Hills CC, Birmingham, Mich.
1962	*Jack Nicklaus (71)	283	Arnold Palmer (74)	Oakmont CC, Oakmont, Pa.
1963	*Julius Boros (70)	293	Jacky Cupit (73) Arnold Palmer (76)	The Country Club, Brookline, Mass.
1964	Ken Venturi	278	Tommy Jacobs	Congressional CC, Bethesda, Md.
1965	*Gary Player (71)	282	Kel Nagle (74)	Bellerive CC, St. Louis, Mo.
1966	*Billy Casper (69)	278	Arnold Palmer (73)	The Olympic Club, San Francisco, Calif.
1967	Jack Nicklaus	275	Arnold Palmer	Baltusrol GC, Springfield, N.J.
1968	Lee Trevino	275	Jack Nicklaus	Oak Hill CC, Rochester, N.Y.
1969	Orville Moody	281	Deane Beman Al Geiberger Bob Rosburg	Champions GC, Houston, Texas
1970	Tony Jacklin	281	Dave Hill	Hazeltine National GC, Chaska, Minn.
1971	*Lee Trevino (68)	280	Jack Nicklaus (71)	Merion GC, Ardmore, Pa.
1972	Jack Nicklaus	290	Bruce Crampton	Pebble Beach GL, Pebble Beach, Calif.
1973	Johnny Miller	279	John Schlee	Oakmont CC, Oakmont, Pa.
1974	Hale Irwin	287	Forrest Fezler	Winged Foot GC, Mamaroneck, N.Y.

Date	Winner	Score	Runner-Up	Venue
1975	*Lou Graham (71)	287	John Mahaffey (73)	Medinah CC, Medinah, Ill.
1976	Jerry Pate	277	Tom Weiskopf Al Geiberger	Atlanta Athletic Club, Duluth, Ga.
1977	Hubert Green	278	Lou Graham	Southern Hills CC, Tulsa, Okla.
1978	Andy North	285	Dave Stockton J.C. Snead	Cherry Hills CC, Englewood, Col.
1979	Hale Irwin	284	Gary Player Jerry Pate	Inverness Club, Toledo, Ohio
1980	Jack Nicklaus	272	Isao Aoki	Baltusrol GC, Springfield, N.J.
1981	David Graham	273	George Burns Bill Rogers	Merion GC, Ardmore, Pa.
1982	Tom Watson	282	Jack Nicklaus	Pebble Beach GL, Pebble Beach, Calif.
1983	Larry Nelson	280	Tom Watson	Oakmont CC, Oakmont, Pa.
1984	*Fuzzy Zoeller (67)	276	Greg Norman (75)	Winged Foot GC, Mamaroneck, N.Y.
1985	Andy North	279	Dave Barr Chen Tze Chung Denis Watson	Oakland Hills CC, Birmingham, Mich.
1986	Raymond Floyd	279	Lanny Wadkins Chip Beck	Shinnecock Hills GC, Southampton, N.Y.
1987	Scott Simpson	277	Tom Watson	The Olympic Club, San Francisco, Calif.
1988	*Curtis Strange (71)	278	Nick Faldo (75)	The Country Club, Brookline, Mass.
1989	Curtis Strange	278	Chip Beck Mark McCumber Ian Woosnam	Oak Hill CC, Rochester, N.Y.
1990	*Hale Irwin (74+3)	280	Mike Donald (74+4)	Medinah CC, Medinah, Ill.
1991	*Payne Stewart (75)	282	Scott Simpson (77)	Hazeltine National GC, Chaska, Minn.
1992	Tom Kite	285	Jeff Sluman	Pebble Beach GL, Pebble Beach, Calif.
1993	Lee Janzen	272	Payne Stewart	Baltusrol GC, Springfield, N.J.
1994	*Ernie Els (74+4+4)	279	Loren Roberts (74+4+5) Colin Montgomerie (78)	Oakmont CC, Oakmont, Pa.
1995	Corey Pavin	280	Greg Norman	Shinnecock Hills GC, Southampton, N.Y.
1996	Steve Jones	278	Tom Lehman Davis Love III	Oakland Hills CC, Birmingham, Mich.
1997	Ernie Els	276	Colin Montgomerie	Congressional CC, Bethesda, Md.
1998	Lee Janzen	280	Payne Stewart	The Olympic Club, San Francisco, Calif.
1999	Payne Stewart	279	Phil Mickelson	Pinehurst No. 2, Pinehurst, N.C.
2000	Tiger Woods	272	Miguel Angel Jimenez Ernie Els	Pebble Beach GL, Pebble Beach, Calif.
2001	*Retief Goosen (70)	276	Mark Brooks (72)	Southern Hills CC, Tulsa, Okla.
2002	Tiger Woods	277	Phil Mickelson	Bethpage State Park, Farmingdale, N.Y.
2003	Jim Furyk	272	Stephen Leaney	Olympia Fields CC, Olympia Fields, Ill.
2004	Retief Goosen	276	Phil Mickelson	Shinnecock Hills GC, Southampton, N.Y.
2005	Michael Campbell	280	Tiger Woods	Pinehurst No. 2, Pinehurst, N.C.

*Winner in playoff; figures in parentheses indicate scores

105th U.S. OPEN Championship Records

Oldest champion (years/months/days)
  45/0/15 — Hale Irwin (1990)
Youngest champion
  19/10/14 — John J. McDermott (1911)
Most victories
  4 — Willie Anderson (1901, '03, '04, '05)
  4 — Robert T. Jones Jr. (1923, '26, '29, '30)
  4 — Ben Hogan (1948, '50, '51, '53)
  4 — Jack Nicklaus (1962, '67, '72, '80)
  3 — Hale Irwin (1974, '79, '90)
  2 — by 16 players: Alex Smith (1906, '10), John J. McDermott (1911, '12), Walter Hagen (1914, '19), Gene Sarazen (1922, '32), Ralph Guldahl (1937, '38), Cary Middlecoff (1949, '56), Julius Boros (1952, '63), Billy Casper (1959, '66), Lee Trevino (1968, '71), Andy North (1978, '85), Curtis Strange (1988, '89), Ernie Els (1994, '97), Lee Janzen (1993, '98), Payne Stewart (1991, '99), Tiger Woods (2000, '02) and Retief Goosen (2001, '04).
Consecutive victories
  Willie Anderson (1903, '04, '05)
  John J. McDermott (1911, '12)
  Robert T. Jones Jr. (1929, '30)
  Ralph Guldahl (1937, '38)
  Ben Hogan (1950, '51)
  Curtis Strange (1988, '89)
Most times runner-up
  4 — Sam Snead
  4 — Robert T. Jones Jr.
  4 — Arnold Palmer
  4 — Jack Nicklaus
Longest course
  7,214 yards — Bethpage State Park (Black Course), Farmingdale, N.Y. (2002) and Pinehurst No. 2, Pinehurst, N.C. (2005)
Shortest course
  Since World War II
  6,528 yards — Merion GC (East Course), Ardmore, Pa. (1971, '81)
Most often host club of Open
  7 — Baltusrol GC, Springfield, N.J. (1903, '15, '36, '54, '67, '80, '93)
  7 — Oakmont (Pa.) CC (1927, '35, '53, '62, '73, '83, '94)
Largest entry
  9,048 (2005)
Smallest entry
  11 (1895)
Lowest score, 72 holes
  272 — Jack Nicklaus (63-71-70-68), at Baltusrol GC (Lower Course), Springfield, N.J. (1980)
  272 — Lee Janzen (67-67-69-69), at Baltusrol GC (Lower Course), Springfield, N.J. (1993)
  272 — Tiger Woods (65-69-71-67), at Pebble Beach GL, Pebble Beach, Calif. (2000)
  272 — Jim Furyk (67-66-67-72), at Olympia Fields CC (North Course), Olympia Fields, Ill. (2003)
Lowest score, first 54 holes
  200 — Jim Furyk (67-66-67), at Olympia Fields CC (North Course), Olympia Fields, Ill. (2003)
Lowest score, last 54 holes
  203 — Loren Roberts (69-64-70), at Oakmont CC, Oakmont, Pa. (1994)
Lowest score, first 36 holes
  133 — Vijay Singh (70-63), at Olympia Fields CC (North Course), Olympia Fields, Ill. (2003)
  133 — Jim Furyk (67-66), at Olympia Fields CC (North Course), Olympia Fields, Ill. (2003)
Lowest score, last 36 holes
  132 — Larry Nelson (65-67), at Oakmont CC, Oakmont, Pa. (1983)
Lowest score, 9 holes
  29 — Neal Lancaster (second nine, fourth round) at Shinnecock Hills GC, Southampton, N.Y. (1995)
  29 — Neal Lancaster (second nine, second round) at Oakland Hills CC, Birmingham, Mich. (1996)
  29 — Vijay Singh (second nine, second round), at Olympia Fields CC (North Course), Olympia Fields, Ill. (2003)
Lowest score, 18 holes
  63 — Johnny Miller, fourth round at Oakmont CC, Oakmont, Pa. (1973)
  63 — Jack Nicklaus, first round at Baltusrol GC (Lower Course), Springfield, N.J. (1980)
  63 — Tom Weiskopf, first round at Baltusrol GC (Lower Course), Springfield, N.J. (1980)
  63 — Vijay Singh, second round at Olympia Fields CC (North Course), Olympia Fields, Ill. (2003)
Largest winning margin
  15 — Tiger Woods (272), at Pebble Beach GL, Pebble Beach Calif. (2000)
Highest winning score
  Since World War II
  293 — Julius Boros, at The Country Club, Brookline, Mass. (1963) (won in playoff)
Best start by champion
  63 — Jack Nicklaus, at Baltusrol GC (Lower Course), Springfield, N.J. (1980)
Best finish by champion
  63 — Johnny Miller, at Oakmont (Pa.) CC (1973)

Worst start by champion
Since World War II
76 — Ben Hogan, at Oakland Hills CC (South Course), Birmingham, Mich. (1951)
76 — Jack Fleck, at The Olympic Club (Lake Course), San Francisco, Calif. (1955)

Worst finish by champion
Since World War II
75 — Cary Middlecoff, at Medinah CC (No. 3 Course), Medinah, Ill. (1949)
75 — Hale Irwin, at Inverness Club, Toledo, Ohio (1979)

Lowest score to lead field, 18 holes
63 — Jack Nicklaus and Tom Weiskopf, at Baltusrol GC (Lower Course), Springfield, N.J. (1980)

Lowest score to lead field, 36 holes
133 — Vijay Singh (70-63) and Jim Furyk (67-66), at Olympia Fields CC (North Course), Olympia Fields, Ill. (2003)

Lowest score to lead field, 54 holes
200 — Jim Furyk (67-66-67), at Olympia Fields CC (North Course), Olympia Fields, Ill. (2003)

Highest score to lead field, 18 holes
Since World War II
71 — Sam Snead, at Oakland Hills CC (South Course), Birmingham, Mich. (1951)
71 — Tommy Bolt, Julius Boros, and Dick Metz, at Southern Hills CC, Tulsa, Okla. (1958)
71 — Tony Jacklin, at Hazeltine National GC, Chaska, Minn. (1970)
71 — Orville Moody, Jack Nicklaus, Chi Chi Rodriguez, Mason Rudolph, Tom Shaw, and Kermit Zarley, at Pebble Beach (Calif.) Golf Links (1972)

Highest score to lead field, 36 holes
Since World War II
144 — Bobby Locke (73-71), at Oakland Hills CC (South Course), Birmingham, Mich. (1951)
144 — Tommy Bolt (67-77) and E. Harvie Ward (74-70), at The Olympic Club (Lake Course), San Francisco, Calif. (1955)
144 — Homero Blancas (74-70), Bruce Crampton (74-70), Jack Nicklaus (71-73), Cesar Seduno (72-72), Lanny Wadkins (76-68) and Kermit Zarley (71-73), at Pebble Beach (Calif.) Golf Links (1972)

Highest score to lead field, 54 holes
Since World War II
218 — Bobby Locke (73-71-74), at Oakland Hills CC (South Course), Birmingham, Mich. (1951)
218 — Jacky Cupit (70-72-76), at The Country Club, Brookline, Mass. (1963)

Lowest 36-hole cut
143 — at Olympia Fields CC (North Course), Olympia Fields, Ill. (2003)

Highest 36-hole cut
155 — at The Olympic Club (Lakeside Course), San Francisco, Calif. (1955)

Most players to tie for lead, 18 holes
7 — at Pebble Beach (Calif.) Golf Links (1972); at Southern Hills CC, Tulsa, Okla. (1977); and at Shinnecock Hills GC, Southampton, N.Y. (1896)

Most players to tie for lead, 36 holes
6 — at Pebble Beach (Calif.) Golf Links (1972)

Most players to tie for lead, 54 holes
4 — at Oakmont (Pa.) CC (1973)

Most sub-par rounds, championship
124 — at Medinah CC (No. 3 Course), Medinah, Ill. (1990)

Most sub-par 72-hole totals, championship
28 — at Medinah CC (No. 3 Course), Medinah, Ill. (1990)

Most sub-par scores, first round
39 — at Medinah CC (No. 3 Course), Medinah, Ill. (1990)

Most sub-par scores, second round
47 — at Medinah CC (No. 3 Course), Medinah, Ill. (1990)

Most sub-par scores, third round
24 — at Medinah CC (No. 3 Course), Medinah, Ill. (1990)

Most sub-par scores, fourth round
18 — at Baltusrol GC (Lower Course), Springfield, N.J. (1993)

Most sub-par rounds by one player in one championship
4 — Billy Casper, at The Olympic Club (Lakeside Course), San Francisco, Calif. (1966)
4 — Lee Trevino, at Oak Hill CC (East Course), Rochester, N.Y. (1968)
4 — Tony Jacklin, at Hazeltine National GC, Chaska, Minn. (1970)
4 — Lee Janzen, at Baltusrol GC (Lower Course), Springfield, N.J. (1993)

Highest score, one hole
19 — Ray Ainsley, at the 16th (par 4) at Cherry Hills CC, Englewood, Col. (1938)

Most consecutive birdies
6 — George Burns (holes 2–7), at Pebble Beach (Calif.) Golf Links (1972) and Andy Dillard (holes 1–6), at Pebble Beach (Calif.) Golf Links (1992)

Most consecutive 3s
7 — Hubert Green (holes 10–16), at Southern Hills Country Club, Tulsa, Okla. (1977)
7 — Peter Jacobsen (holes 1–7), at The Country Club, Brookline, Mass. (1988)

Most consecutive Opens
44 — Jack Nicklaus (1957-2000)

Most Opens completed 72 holes
35 — Jack Nicklaus

Most consecutive Opens completed 72 holes
22 — Walter Hagen (1913-36; no Championships 1917-18)
22 — Gene Sarazen (1920-41)
22 — Gary Player (1958-79)

Robert Sommers is the former editor and publisher of the USGA's *Golf Journal*, author of *The U.S. Open: Golf's Ultimate Challenge* and *Golf Anecdotes*. He is based in Port St. Lucie, Fla.

The photographers and technicians of **Getty Images** who contributed to this publication are **Rebecca Butala, David Cannon, Scott Halleran, Ross Kinnaird, Streeter Lecka, Andy Lyons, Donald Miralle** and **Jamie Squire**.

105th U.S. Open Championship

Pinehurst No. 2

June 16-19, 2005

Par and Yardage

Hole	Par	Yardage	Hole	Par	Yardage
1	4	401	10	5	607
2	4	469	11	4	476
3	4	336	12	4	449
4	5	565	13	4	378
5	4	472	14	4	468
6	3	220	15	3	203
7	4	404	16	4	492
8	4	467	17	3	190
9	3	175	18	4	442
	35	3,509		35	3,705